A. W. Pink Books

THE
ATTRIBUTES
OF
GOD

Table of Contents

Chapter 1 – The Solitariness of God..3
Chapter 2 – The Decrees of God..7
Chapter 3 – The Knowledge of God...11
Chapter 4 – The Foreknowledge of God..15
Chapter 5 – The Supremacy of God..21
Chapter 6 – The Sovereignty of God...25
Chapter 7 – The Immutability of God..30
Chapter 8 – The Holiness of God..34
Chapter 9 – The Power of God...39
Chapter 10 – The Faithfulness of God..45
Chapter 11 – The Goodness of God...50
Chapter 12 – The Patience of God...54
Chapter 13 – The Grace of God...58
Chapter 14 – The Mercy of God...63
Chapter 15 – The Loving-kindness of God.....................................68
Chapter 16 – The Love of God...72
Chapter 17 – The Wrath of God...81
Chapter 18 – The Contemplation of God.......................................86
Chapter 19 – The Bounties of God..90
Chapter 20 – The Gifts of God...94
Chapter 21 – The Guidance of God...98
Chapter 22 – The Blessings of God...119
Chapter 23 – The Cursings of God..123
Chapter 24 – The Gospel of the Grace of God............................127

CHAPTER 1
The Solitariness of God

The title of this article is perhaps not sufficiently explicit to indicate its theme. This is partly due to the fact that so few today are accustomed to meditate upon the personal perfections of God. Comparatively few of those who occasionally read the Bible are aware of the awe-inspiring and worship-provoking grandeur of the divine character. That God is great in wisdom, wondrous in power, yet full of mercy, is assumed by many to be almost common knowledge; but, to entertain anything approaching an adequate conception of His being, His nature, and His attributes, as these are revealed in Holy Scripture, is something which very, very few people in these degenerate times have attained unto. God is solitary in His excellency. "Who is like unto You, O Lord, among the gods? who is like You, glorious in holiness, fearful in praises, doing wonders?" (Exo 15:11).

"In the beginning God" (Gen 1:1). There was a time, if "time" it could be called, when God, in the unity of His nature (though subsisting equally in three divine persons), dwelt all alone. "In the beginning God." There was no heaven, where His glory is now particularly manifested. There was no earth to engage His attention. There were no angels to hymn His praises; no universe to be upheld by the word of His power. There was nothing, no one, but God; and that, not for a day, a year, or an age, but "from everlasting." During eternity past, God was alone: self-contained, self-sufficient, self-satisfied; in need of nothing. Had a universe, had angels, had human beings been necessary to Him in any way, they also had been called into existence from all eternity. The creating of them when He did, added nothing to God essentially. He changes not (Mal 3:6), therefore His essential glory can be neither augmented nor diminished.

God was under no constraint, no obligation, no necessity to create. That He chose to do so was purely a sovereign act on His part, caused by nothing outside Himself, determined by nothing but His own mere good pleasure; for He "works all things after the counsel of His own will" (Eph 1:11). That He did create was simply for His manifestative glory. Do some of our readers

3

imagine that we have gone beyond what Scripture warrants? Then our appeal shall be to the Law and the Testimony: "Stand up and bless the Lord your God forever and ever: and blessed be Your glorious name, which is exalted above all blessing and praise" (Neh 9:5). God is no gainer even from our worship. He was in no need of that external glory of His grace which arises from His redeemed, for He is glorious enough in Himself without that. What was it that moved Him to predestinate His elect to the glory of His grace? It was, as Ephesians 1:5 tells us, "according to the good pleasure of His will."

We are well aware that the high ground we are here treading is new and strange to almost all of our readers; for that reason it is well to move slowly. Let our appeal again be to the Scriptures. At the end of Romans 11, where the Apostle brings to a close his argument on salvation by pure and sovereign grace, he asks, "For who has known the mind of the Lord? Or who has been His counselor? Or who has first given to Him, and it shall be recompensed unto him again?" (vv. 34-35). The force of this is, it is impossible to bring the Almighty under obligations to the creature; God gains nothing from us. "If you are righteous, what do you give to him, or what does he receive from your hand? Your wickedness affects only a man like yourself, and your righteousness only the sons of men" (Job 35:7-8), but it certainly cannot affect God, who is all-blessed in Himself. "So you also, when you have done everything you were told to do, should say—We are unworthy servants; we have only done our duty." (Luke 17:10)—our obedience has profited God nothing.

Nay, we go further; our Lord Jesus Christ added nothing to God in His essential being and glory, either by what He did or suffered. True, blessedly and gloriously true, He manifested the glory of God to us, but He added nothing to God. He Himself expressly declares so, and there is no appeal from His words: "My goodness extends not to You" (Psalm 16:2). The whole of that Psalm is a Psalm of Christ. Christ's goodness or righteousness reached unto His saints in the earth (v.3), but God was high above and beyond it all. God alone is "the Blessed One" (Mark 14:61, Greek).

It is perfectly true that God is both honored and dishonored by men; not in His essential being, but in His official character. It is equally true that God has been "glorified" by creation, by providence, and by redemption. This we do not and dare not dispute for a moment. But all of this has to do with His manifest glory and the recognition of it by us. Yet had God so pleased He might have continued alone for all eternity, without making known His glory unto creatures. Whether He should do so or not was determined solely by His own will. He was perfectly blessed in Himself before the first creature was called into being. And what are all the creatures of His hands unto Him even now? Let Scripture again make answer:

"Surely the nations are like a drop in a bucket; they are regarded as dust on the scales; he weighs the islands as though they were fine dust. Lebanon is not sufficient for altar fires, nor its animals enough for burnt offerings. Before him all the nations are as nothing; they are regarded by him as worthless and less than nothing. To whom, then, will you compare God? What image will you compare him to?" (Isa 40:15-18). That is the God of Scripture; alas, He is still "the unknown God" (Acts 17:23) to the heedless multitudes.

"He sits enthroned above the circle of the earth, and its people are like grasshoppers. He stretches out the heavens like a canopy, and spreads them out like a tent to live in. He brings princes to naught and reduces the rulers of this world to nothing." (Isa 40:22,23). How vastly different is the God of Scripture from the "God" of the average pulpit!

Nor is the testimony of the New Testament any different from that of the Old: how could it be, seeing that both have one and the same Author! There do we read, "God, the blessed and only Ruler, the King of kings and Lord of lords, who alone is immortal and who lives in unapproachable light, whom no one has seen or can see. To him be honor and might forever. Amen" (1 Tim 6:15,16).

Such an One is to be revered, worshiped, adored. He is solitary in His majesty, unique in His excellency, peerless in His perfections. He sustains all, but is Himself independent of all. He gives to all, but is enriched by none.

Such a God cannot be found out by searching. He can be known only as He is revealed to the heart by the Holy Spirit through the Word. It is true that creation demonstrates a Creator so plainly that men are "without excuse"; yet, we still have to say with Job, "Lo, these are parts of His ways: but how little a portion is heard of Him? but the thunder of His power who can understand?" (26:14) The so-called argument from design by well-meaning "Apologists" has, we believe, done much more harm than good, for it has attempted to bring down the great God to the level of finite comprehension, and thereby has lost sight of His solitary excellence.

Analogy has been drawn between a savage finding a watch upon the sands, and from a close examination of it he infers a watch-maker. So far so good. But attempt to go further: suppose that savage sits down on the sand and endeavors to form to himself a conception of this watch-maker, his personal affections and manners; his disposition, acquirements, and moral character—all that goes to make up a personality; could he ever think or reason out a real man—the man who made the watch, so that he could say, "I am acquainted with him"? It seems trifling to ask such questions, but is the eternal and infinite God so much more within the grasp of human reason? No, indeed. The God of Scripture can only be known by those to whom He makes Himself known.

Nor is God known by the intellect. "God is Spirit" (John 4:24), and therefore can only be known spiritually. But fallen man is not spiritual; he is carnal. He is dead to all that is spiritual. Unless he is born again, supernaturally brought from death unto life, miraculously translated out of darkness into light, he cannot even see the things of God (John 3:3), still less apprehend them (1 Cor 2:14). The Holy Spirit has to shine in our hearts (not intellects) in order to give us "the knowledge of the glory of God in the face of Jesus Christ" (2 Cor 4:6). And even that spiritual knowledge is but fragmentary. The regenerated soul has to grow in grace and in the knowledge of the Lord Jesus (2 Peter 3:18).

The principal prayer and aim of Christians should be that we "walk worthy of the Lord unto all pleasing, being fruitful in every good work, and increasing in the knowledge of God" (Col 1:10).

CHAPTER 2
The Decrees of God

The decree of God is His purpose or determination with respect to future things. We have used the singular number as Scripture does (Rom 8:28; Eph 3:11), because there was only one act of His infinite mind about future things. But we speak as if there had been many, because our minds are only capable of thinking of successive revolutions, as thoughts and occasions arise, or in reference to the various objects of His decree, which being many seem to us to require a distinct purpose for each one. But an infinite understanding does not proceed by steps, from one stage to another: "Known unto God are all His works from the beginning of the world" (Acts 15:18).

The Scriptures make mention of the decrees of God in many passages, and under a variety of terms. The word "decree" is found in Psalm 2:7. In Ephesians 3:11 we read of His "eternal purpose." In Acts 2:23 of His "determinate counsel and foreknowledge." In Ephesians 1:9 of the mystery of His "will." In Romans 8:29 that He also did "predestinate." In Ephesians 1:9 of His good pleasure." God's decrees are called His "counsel" to signify they are consummately wise. They are called God's "will" to show He was under no control, but acted according to His own pleasure. When a man's will is the rule of his conduct, it is usually capricious and unreasonable; but wisdom is always associated with "will" in the divine proceedings, and accordingly, God's decrees are said to be "the counsel of His own will" (Eph 1:11).

The decrees of God relate to all future things without exception: whatever is done in time was foreordained before time began. God's purpose was concerned with everything, whether great or small, whether good or evil, although with reference to the latter we must be careful to state that while God is the Orderer and Controller of sin, He is not the Author of it in the same way that He is the Author of good. Sin could not proceed from a holy God by positive and direct creation, but only by decretive permission and negative action. God's decree is as comprehensive as His government, extending to all creatures and all events. It was concerned about our life and death; about our state in time, and our state in eternity. As God works all things after the counsel of His own will, we learn from His works what His counsel was, as we judge of an architect's plan by inspecting the building which was erected under his directions.

God did not merely decree to make man, place him upon the earth, and then leave him to his own uncontrolled guidance; instead, He fixed all the circumstances in the lot of individuals, and all the particulars which will comprise the history of the human race from its commencement to its close. He did not merely decree that general laws should be established for the government of the world, but He settled the application of those laws to all particular cases. Our days are numbered, and so are the hairs of our heads. We may learn what is the extent of the divine decrees from the dispensations of providence, in which they are executed. The care of Providence reaches to the most insignificant creatures, and the most minute events—the death of a sparrow, and the fall of a hair. Let us now consider some of the PROPERTIES of the divine decrees.

First, they are eternal. To suppose any of them to be made in time is to suppose that some new occasion has occurred; some unforeseen event or combination of circumstances has arisen, which has induced the Most High to form a new resolution. This would argue that the knowledge of the Deity is limited, and that He is growing wiser in the progress of time—which would be horrible blasphemy. No man who believes that the divine understanding is infinite, comprehending the past, the present, and the future, will ever assent to the erroneous doctrine of temporal decrees. God is not ignorant of future events which will be executed by human volitions; He has foretold them in innumerable instances, and prophecy is but the manifestation of His eternal prescience. Scripture affirms that believers were chosen in Christ before the world began (Eph 1:4), yes, that grace was "given" to them then (2 Tim 1:9).

Secondly, the decrees of God are wise. Wisdom is shown in the selection of the best possible ends and of the fittest means of accomplishing them. That this character belongs to the decrees of God is evident from what we know of them. They are disclosed to us by their execution, and every proof of wisdom in the works of God is a proof of the wisdom of the plan, in conformity to which they are performed. As the Psalmist declared, "O Lord, how manifold are Your works! in wisdom have You made them all" (104:24). It is indeed but a very small part of them which falls under our observation, yet, we ought to proceed here as we do in other cases, and judge of the whole by the specimen, of what is unknown, by what is known. He who perceives the workings of admirable skill in the parts of a machine which he has an opportunity to examine, is naturally led to believe that the other parts are equally admirable. In like manner we should satisfy our minds as to God's works when doubts intrude themselves upon us, and repel any objections that may be suggested by something that we cannot reconcile to our notions of what is good and wise. When we reach the bounds of the finite and gaze toward the mysterious realm of the infinite, let us exclaim, "O the depth of the riches both of the wisdom and knowledge of God!" (Rom 11:33).

Thirdly, they are free. "Who has directed the Spirit of the Lord, or being His counselor has taught Him? With whom took He counsel, and who instructed Him, and taught Him in the path of judgment, and taught Him knowledge, and showed to Him the way of understanding?" (Isa 40:13-14). God was alone when He made His decrees, and His determinations were influenced by no external cause. He was free to decree or not to decree, and to decree one thing and not another. This liberty we must ascribe to Him who is Supreme, Independent, and Sovereign in all His doings.

Fourthly, they are absolute and unconditional. The execution of them is not suspended upon any condition which may, or may not be, performed. In every instance where God has decreed an end, He has also decreed every means to that end. The One who decreed the salvation of His elect also decreed to work faith in them (2 Thess 2:13). "My counsel shall stand, and I will do all My pleasure" (Isa 46:10): but that could not be, if His counsel depended upon a condition which might not be performed. But God "works all things after the counsel of His own will" (Eph 1:11).

Side by side with the immutability and invincibility of God's decrees, Scripture plainly teaches that man is a responsible creature and answerable for his actions. And if our thoughts are formed from God's Word, the maintenance of the one will not lead to the denial of the other. That there is a real difficulty in defining where the one ends and the other begins, is freely granted. This is ever the case where there is a conjunction of the divine and the human. Real prayer is incited by the Spirit, yet it is also the cry of a human heart. The Scriptures are the inspired Word of God, yet they were written by men who were something more than machines in the hand of the Spirit. Christ is both God and man. He is Omniscient, yet "increased in wisdom" (Luke 2:52). He was Almighty, yet was "crucified through weakness" (2 Cor 13:4). He was the Prince of life, yet He died. High mysteries are these, yet faith receives them unquestioningly.

It has often been pointed out in the past that every objection made against the eternal decrees of God applies with equal force against His eternal foreknowledge. "Whether God has decreed all things that ever come to pass or not, all that own the being of a God, own that He knows all things beforehand. Now, it is self-evident that if He knows all things beforehand, He either does approve of them or does not approve of them; that is, He either is willing they should be, or He is not willing they should be. But to will that they should be is to decree them" (Jonathan Edwards).

Finally, attempt, with me, to assume and then to contemplate the opposite. To deny the divine decrees would be to predicate a world and all its concerns regulated by undesigned chance or blind fate. Then what peace, what assurance, what comfort would there be for our poor hearts and minds? What refuge would there be to fly to in the hour of need and trial? None at all. There would be nothing better than the black darkness and abject horror of atheism. O my reader, how thankful should we be that everything is determined by infinite wisdom and goodness! What praise and gratitude are due unto God for His divine decrees. It is because of them that "we know that all things work together for good to those who love God, to those who are the called according to His purpose" (Rom 8:28).

Well may we exclaim, "For of Him, and through Him, and to Him, are all things: to Whom be glory forever. Amen" (Rom 11:36).

CHAPTER 3
The Knowledge of God

God is omniscient. He knows everything: everything possible, everything actual; all events and all creatures, of the past, the present, and the future. He is perfectly acquainted with every detail in the life of every being in heaven, in earth, and in hell. "He knows what is in the darkness" (Dan 2:22). Nothing escapes His notice, nothing can be hidden from Him, nothing is forgotten by Him. Well may we say with the Psalmist, "Such knowledge is too wonderful for me; it is high, I cannot attain unto it" (Psalm 139:6). His knowledge is perfect. He never errs, never changes, never overlooks anything. "Neither is there any creature that is not manifest in His sight: but all things are naked and opened unto the eyes of Him with whom we have to do" (Heb 4:13). Yes, such is the God "with whom we have to do!"

"You know when I sit and when I rise; you perceive my thoughts from afar. You discern my going out and my lying down; you are familiar with all my ways. Before a word is on my tongue you know it completely, O Lord" (Psalm 139:2-4). What a wondrous Being is the God of Scripture! Each of His glorious attributes should render Him honorable in our esteem. The apprehension of His omniscience ought to bow us in adoration before Him. Yet how little do we meditate upon this divine perfection! Is it because the very thought of it fills us with uneasiness?

How solemn is this fact: nothing can be concealed from God! "For I know the things that come into your mind, everyone of them" (Eze 11:5). Though He is invisible to us, we are not so to Him. Neither the darkness of night, the closest curtains, nor the deepest dungeon can hide any sinner from the eyes of Omniscience. The trees of the garden were not able to conceal our first parents. No human eye beheld Cain murder his brother, but his Maker witnessed his crime. Sarah might laugh derisively in the seclusion of her tent, yet was it heard by Jehovah. Achan stole a wedge of gold and carefully hid it in the earth, but God brought it to light. David was at much pains to cover up his wickedness, but before long the all-seeing God sent one of His servants to say to him, "You are the man!" And to writer and reader is also said, "Be sure your sin will find you out" (Num 32:23).

Men would strip Deity of His omniscience if they could—what a proof that "the carnal mind is enmity against God!" (Rom 8:7) The wicked do as naturally hate this divine perfection as much as they are naturally compelled to acknowledge it. They wish there might be no Witness of their sins, no Searcher of their hearts, no Judge of their deeds. They seek to banish such a God from their thoughts: "They consider not in their hearts that I remember all their wickedness" (Hosea 7:2). How solemn is Psalm 90:8! Good reason has every Christ-rejecter for trembling before it: "You have set our iniquities before You, our secret sins in the light of Your countenance."

But to the believer, the fact of God's omniscience is a truth fraught with much comfort. In times of perplexity he says with job, "But He knows the way that I take" (23:10). It may be profoundly mysterious to me, quite incomprehensible to my friends, but "He knows!" In times of weariness and weakness believers assure themselves, "He knows our frame; He remembers that we are dust" (Psalm 103:14). In times of doubt and suspicion they appeal to this very attribute, saying, "Search me, O God, and know my heart: try me, and know my thoughts: and see if there be any wicked way in me, and lead me in the way everlasting" (Psalm 139:23,24). In time of sad failure, when our actions have belied our hearts, when our deeds have repudiated our devotion, and the searching question comes to us, "So you love you Me?", we say, as Peter did, "Lord, You know all things; You know that I love You" (John 21:17).

Here is encouragement to prayer. There is no cause for fearing that the petitions of the righteous will not be heard, or that their sighs and tears shall escape the notice of God, since He knows the thoughts and intents of the heart. There is no danger of the individual saint being overlooked amidst the multitude of supplicants who daily and hourly present their various petitions, for an infinite Mind is as capable of paying the same attention to millions as if only one individual were seeking its attention. So too the lack of appropriate language, the inability to give expression to the deepest longing of the soul, will not jeopardize our prayers, for "It shall come to pass, that before they call, I will answer; and while they are yet speaking, I will hear" (Isa 65:24).

"Great is our Lord, and of great power: His understanding is infinite" (Psalm 147:5). God not only knows whatever has happened in the past in every part of His vast domains, and He is not only thoroughly acquainted with everything that is now transpiring throughout the entire universe, but He is also perfectly cognizant of every event, from the least to the greatest, that ever will happen in the ages to come. God's knowledge of the future is as complete as is His knowledge of the past and the present, and that, because the future depends entirely upon Himself. Were it in any ways possible for something to occur apart from either the direct agency or permission of God, then that something would be independent of Him, and He would at once cease to be Supreme.

Now the divine knowledge of the future is not a mere abstraction, but something which is inseparably connected with and accompanied by His purpose. God has Himself designed whatever shall yet be, and what He has designed must be effectuated. As His most sure Word affirms, "He does according to His will in the army of heaven, and among the inhabitants of the earth: and none can stay His hand" (Dan 4:35). And again, "There are many devices in a man's heart; nevertheless the counsel of the Lord, that shall stand" (Pro 19:21). The wisdom and power of God being alike infinite, the accomplishment of whatever He has purposed is absolutely guaranteed. It is no more possible for the divine counsels to fail in their execution than it would be for the thrice holy God to lie.

Nothing relating to the future is in any ways uncertain so far as the actualization of God's counsels are concerned. None of His decrees are left contingent either on creatures or secondary causes. There is no future event which is only a mere possibility, that is, something which may or may not come to pass: "Known unto God are all His works from the beginning" (Acts 15:18). Whatever God has decreed is inexorably certain, for He is without variableness, or shadow of turning" (James 1:17). Therefore we are told at the very beginning of that book, which unveils to us so much of the future, of "Things which must shortly come to pass" (Rev 1:1).

The perfect knowledge of God is exemplified and illustrated in every prophecy recorded in His Word. In the Old Testament are to be found scores of predictions concerning the history of Israel, which were fulfilled to their minutest detail, centuries after they were made. In them too are scores more foretelling the earthly career of Christ, and they too were accomplished literally and perfectly. Such prophecies could only have been given by One who knew the end from the beginning, and whose knowledge rested upon the unconditional certainty of the accomplishment of everything foretold. In like manner, both Old and New Testament contain many other announcements yet future, and they too "must be fulfilled" (Luke 24:44), must because foretold by Him who decreed them.

It should, however, be pointed out that neither God's knowledge nor His cognition of the future, considered simply in themselves, are causative. Nothing has ever come to pass, or ever will, merely because God knew it. The cause of all things is the will of God. The man who really believes the Scriptures knows beforehand that the seasons will continue to follow each other with unfailing regularity to the end of earth's history (Gen 8:22), yet his knowledge is not the cause of their succession. So God's knowledge does not arise from things because they are or will be, but because He has ordained them to be. God knew and foretold the crucifixion of His Son many hundreds of years before He became incarnate, and this, because in the divine purpose, He was a Lamb slain from the foundation of the world: hence we read of His being "delivered by the determinate counsel and foreknowledge of God" (Acts 2:23).

A word or two by way of application.
The infinite knowledge of God should fill us with amazement. How far exalted above the wisest man is the Lord! None of us knows what a day may bring forth, but all futurity is open to His omniscient gaze. The infinite knowledge of God ought to fill us with holy awe. Nothing we do, say, or even think, escapes the cognizance of Him with whom we have to do: "The eyes of the Lord are in every place, beholding the evil and the good" (Pro 15:3). What a curb this would be unto us, did we but meditate upon it more frequently! Instead of acting recklessly, we should say with Hagar, "You God see me" (Gen 16:13). The apprehension of God's infinite knowledge should fill the Christian with adoration. The whole of my life stood open to His view from the beginning. He foresaw my every fall, my every sin, my every backsliding; yet, nevertheless, fixed His heart upon me. Oh, how the realization of this should bow me in wonder and worship before Him!

CHAPTER 4
The Foreknowledge of God

What controversies have been engendered by this subject in the past! But what truth of Holy Scripture is there which has not been made the occasion of theological and ecclesiastical battles? The deity of Christ, His virgin birth, His atoning death, His second advent; the believer's justification, sanctification, security; the church, its organization, officers, discipline; baptism, the Lord's supper and a score of other precious truths might be mentioned. Yet, the controversies which have been waged over them did not close the mouths of God's faithful servants; why, then, should we avoid the vexing question of God's foreknowledge, because, forsooth, there are some who will charge us with fomenting strife? Let others contend if they will, our duty is to bear witness according to the light vouchsafed us.

There are two things concerning the foreknowledge of God about which many are in ignorance: the meaning of the term, and its Scriptural scope. Because this ignorance is so widespread, it is an easy matter for preachers and teachers to palm off perversions of this subject, even upon the people of God. There is only one safeguard against error, and that is to be established in the faith; and for that, there has to be prayerful and diligent study, and a receiving with meekness the engrafted Word of God. Only then are we fortified against the attacks of those who assail us. There are those today who are misusing this very truth in order to discredit and deny the absolute sovereignty of God in the salvation of sinners. Just as higher critics are repudiating the divine inspiration of the Scriptures; evolutionists, the work of God in creation; so some pseudo Bible teachers are perverting His foreknowledge in order to set aside His unconditional election unto eternal life.

When the solemn and blessed subject of divine foreordination is expounded, when God's eternal choice of certain ones to be conformed to the image of His Son is set forth—the enemy sends along some man to argue that election is based upon the foreknowledge of God, and this "foreknowledge" is interpreted to mean that God foresaw certain ones would be more pliable than others, that they would respond more readily to the strivings of the Spirit, and that because God knew they would believe, He accordingly, predestinated them unto salvation. But such a statement is radically wrong. It repudiates the truth of total depravity, for it argues that there is something good in some men. It takes away the independency of God, for it makes His decrees rest upon what He discovers in the creature. It completely turns things upside down, for in saying God foresaw certain sinners would believe in Christ, and that because of this, He predestinated them unto salvation, is the very reverse of the truth. Scripture affirms that God, in His high sovereignty, singled out certain ones to be recipients of His distinguishing favors (Acts 13:48), and therefore He determined to bestow upon them the gift of faith. False theology makes God's foreknowledge of our believing the cause of His election to salvation; whereas, God's election is the cause, and our believing in Christ is the effect.

Before proceeding further with our discussion of this much misunderstood theme, let us pause and define our terms. What is meant by "foreknowledge"? "To know beforehand," is the ready reply of many. But we must not jump to conclusions, nor must we turn to Webster's dictionary as the final court of appeal, for it is not a matter of the etymology of the term employed. What is needed is to find out how the word is used in Scripture. The Holy Spirit's usage of an expression always defines its meaning and scope. It is failure to apply this simple rule which is responsible for so much confusion and error. So many people assume they already know the signification of a certain word used in Scripture, and then they are too dilatory to test their assumptions by means of a concordance. Let us amplify this point.

Take the word "flesh." Its meaning appears to be so obvious that many would regard it as a waste of time to look up its various connections in Scripture. It is hastily assumed that the word is synonymous with the physical body, and so no inquiry is made. But, in fact, "flesh" in Scripture frequently includes far more than what is corporeal; all that is embraced by the term can only be ascertained by a diligent comparison of every occurrence of it and by a study of each separate context. Take the word "world." The average reader of the Bible imagines this word is the equivalent for the human race, and consequently, many passages where the term is found are wrongly interpreted. Take the word "immortality." Surely it requires no study! Obviously it has reference to the indestructibility of the soul. Ah, my reader, it is foolish and wrong to assume anything where the Word of God is concerned. If the reader will take the trouble to carefully examine each passage where "mortal" and "immortal" are found, it will be seen that these words are never applied to the soul, but always to the body.

Now what has been said on "flesh," the "world," "immortality," applies with equal force to the terms "know" and "foreknow." Instead of imagining that these words signify no more than a simple cognition, the different passages in which they occur require to be carefully weighed. The word "foreknowledge" is not found in the Old Testament. But "know" occurs there frequently. When that term is used in connection with God, it often signifies to regard with favor, denoting not mere cognition but an affection for the object in view. "I know you by name" (Exo 33:17). "You have been rebellious against the Lord from the day that I knew you" (Deut 9:24). "Before I formed you in the womb, I knew you" (Jer 1:5). "They have made princes, and I knew it not" (Hosea 8:4). "You only have I known of all the families of the earth" (Amos 3:2). In these passages "knew" signifies either loved or appointed.

In like manner, the word "know" is frequently used in the New Testament, in the same sense as in the Old Testament. "Then will I profess unto them, I never knew you" (Matt 7:23). "I am the good shepherd; I know My sheep and My sheep know Me" (John 10:14). "If any man loves God, the same is known by Him" (1 Cor 8:3). "The Lord knows those who are His" (2 Tim 2:19).

Now the word "foreknowledge" as it is used in the New Testament is less ambiguous than in its simple form "to know." If every passage in which it occurs is carefully studied, it will be discovered that it is a moot point whether it ever has reference to the mere perception of events which are yet to take place. The fact is that "foreknowledge" is never used in Scripture in connection with events or actions; instead, it always has reference to persons. It is persons God is said to "foreknow," not the actions of those persons. In proof of this we shall now quote each passage where this expression is found.

The first occurrence is in Acts 2:23. There we read, "Him being delivered by the determinate counsel and foreknowledge of God, you have taken, and by wicked hands have crucified and slain." If careful attention is paid to the wording of this verse, it will be seen that the Apostle was not there speaking of God's foreknowledge of the act of the crucifixion, but of the Person crucified: "Him [Christ] being delivered by..."

The second occurrence is in Romans 8:29,30. "For those God foreknew he also predestined to be conformed to the likeness of his Son, that he might be the firstborn among many brothers. And those he predestined, he also called; those he called, he also justified; those he justified, he also glorified." Weigh well the pronoun that is used here. It is not what He did foreknow, but those He foreknew. It is not the surrendering of their wills nor the believing of their hearts, but the persons themselves, that are here in view. "God has not cast away His people which He foreknew" (Rom 11:2). Once more the plain reference is to persons, and to persons only.

The last mention is in I Peter 1:2: "Elect according to the foreknowledge of God the Father." Who are "elect according to the foreknowledge of God the Father?" The previous verse tells us: the reference is to the "strangers scattered," that is, the Diaspora, the Dispersion, the believing Jews. Thus, here too the reference is to persons, and not to their foreseen acts.

Now in view of these passages (and there are no more) what Scriptural ground is there for anyone saying God "foreknew" the acts of certain ones, namely, their "repenting and believing," and that because of those acts He elected them unto salvation? The answer is: None whatever! Scripture never speaks of repentance and faith as being foreseen or foreknown by God. Truly, He did know from all eternity that certain ones would repent and believe, yet this is not what Scripture refers to as the object of God's foreknowledge. The word uniformly refers to God's foreknowing persons; then let us "hold fast the form of sound words" (2 Tim 1:13).

Another thing to which we desire to call particular attention is that the first two passages quoted above show plainly and teach implicitly that God's foreknowledge is not causative, that instead, something else lies behind, precedes it, and that something is His own sovereign decree. Christ was "delivered by the [1] determinate counsel and [2] foreknowledge of God" (Acts 2:23). His counsel or decree was the ground of His foreknowledge. So again in Romans 8:29. That verse opens with the word "for," which tells us to look back to what immediately precedes. What, then, does the previous verse say? This: "All things work together for good to them ... who are the called according to His purpose." Thus God's foreknowledge is based upon His "purpose" or decree (see Psalm 2:7).

God foreknows what will be because He has decreed what shall be. It is therefore a reversing of the order of Scripture, a putting of the cart before the horse, to affirm that God elects because He foreknows people. The truth is, He foreknows because He has elected. This removes the ground or cause of election from outside the creature, and places it in God's own sovereign will. God purposed in Himself to elect a certain people, not because of anything good in them or from them, either actual or foreseen, but solely out of His own mere pleasure. As to why He chose the ones He did, we do not know, and can only say, "Yes, Father, for this was Your good pleasure." The plain truth in Romans 8:29 is that God, before the foundation of the world, singled out certain sinners and appointed them unto salvation (2 Thess 2:13). This is clear from the concluding words of the verse: "Predestinate to be conformed to the image of His Son." God did not predestinate those whom He foreknew were conformed," but, on the contrary, those whom He "foreknew" (that is, loved and elected) He predestinated "to be conformed." Their conformity to Christ is not the cause, but the effect of God's foreknowledge and predestination.

God did not elect any sinner because He foresaw that he would believe, for the simple but sufficient reason that no sinner ever does believe until God gives him faith; just as no man sees until God gives him sight. Sight is God's gift, seeing is the consequence of my using His gift. So faith is God's gift (Eph 2:8,9), believing is the consequence of my using His gift. If it were true that God had elected certain ones to be saved because in due time they would believe, then that would make believing a meritorious act, and in that event the saved sinner would have ground for "boasting," which Scripture emphatically denies (Eph 2:9).

Surely God's Word is plain enough in teaching that believing is not a meritorious act. It affirms that Christians are a people who "have believed through grace" (Acts 18:27). If, then, they have believed "through grace," there is absolutely nothing meritorious about "believing," and if nothing meritorious, it could not be the ground or cause which moved God to choose them. No; God's choice proceeds not from anything in us, or anything from us, but solely from His own sovereign pleasure. Once more, in Romans 11:5, we read of "a remnant according to the election of grace." There it is, plain enough; election itself is of grace, and grace is unmerited favor, something for which we had no claim upon God whatever.

It thus appears that it is highly important for us to have clear and spiritual views of the foreknowledge of God. Erroneous conceptions about it lead inevitably to thoughts most dishonoring to Him. The popular idea of divine foreknowledge is altogether inadequate. God not only knew the end from the beginning, but He planned, fixed, predestinated everything from the beginning. And, as cause stands to effect, so God's purpose is the ground of His foreknowledge. If then the reader is a real Christian, he is so because God chose him in Christ before the foundation of the world (Eph 1:4), and chose not because He foresaw you would believe, but chose simply because it pleased Him to choose; chose you notwithstanding your natural unbelief. This being so, all the glory and praise belongs alone to Him. You have no ground for taking any credit to yourself. You have "believed through grace" (Acts 18:27), and that, because your very election was "of grace" (Rom 11:5).

CHAPTER 5
The Supremacy of God

In one of his letters to Erasmus, Luther said, "Your thoughts of God are too human." Probably that renowned scholar resented such a rebuke, the more so, since it proceeded from a miner's son; nevertheless, it was thoroughly deserved. We too, though having no standing among the religious leaders of this degenerate age, give the same charge against the majority of the preachers of our day, and against those who, instead of searching the Scriptures for themselves, lazily accept the teaching of others. The most dishonoring and degrading conceptions of the rule and reign of the Almighty are now held almost everywhere. To countless thousands, even among those professing to be Christians, the God of the Scriptures is quite unknown.

Of old, God complained to an apostate Israel, "You thought I was just like you" (Psalm 50:21). Such must now be His indictment against an apostate Christendom. Men imagine that the Most High is moved by sentiment, rather that actuated by principle. They suppose that His omnipotence is such an idle fiction that Satan is thwarting His designs on every side. They think that if He has formed any plan or purpose at all, then it must be like theirs, constantly subject to change. They openly declare that whatever power He possesses must be restricted, lest He invade the citadel of man's "free will" and reduce him to a "machine." They lower the all-efficacious atonement, which has actually redeemed everyone for whom it was made, to a mere "remedy," which sin-sick souls may use if they feel disposed to; and they enervate the invincible work of the Holy Spirit to an "offer" of the Gospel which sinners may accept or reject as they please.

The god of this twentieth century no more resembles the Supreme Sovereign of Holy Writ, than does the dim flickering of a candle the glory of the midday sun. The god who is now talked about in the average pulpit, spoken of in the ordinary Sunday School, mentioned in much of the religious literature of the day, and preached in most of the so-called Bible Conferences is the figment of human imagination, an invention of mushy sentimentality. The heathen outside of the pale of Christendom form gods out of wood and stone, while the millions of heathen inside Christendom manufacture a god out of their own carnal mind. In reality, they are but atheists, for there is no other possible alternative between an absolutely supreme God, and no God at all. A god whose will is resisted, whose designs are frustrated, whose purpose is checkmated, possesses no title to Deity, and so far from being a fit object of worship, merits nothing but contempt!

The supremacy of the true and living God might well be argued from the infinite distance which separates the mightiest creatures from the almighty Creator. He is the Potter, they are but the clay in His hands, to be molded into vessels of honor, or to be dashed into pieces (Psalm 2:9) as He pleases. Were all the citizens of heaven and all the inhabitants of the earth to combine in revolt against Him, it would occasion Him no uneasiness, and would have less effect upon His eternal and unassailable Throne than has the spray of Mediterranean's waves upon the towering rocks of Gibraltar. So puerile and powerless is the creature to affect the Most High. Scripture itself tells us that when the Gentile heads unite with apostate Israel to defy Jehovah and His Christ, "He who sits in the heavens shall laugh" (Psalm 2:4).

The absolute and universal supremacy of God is plainly and positively affirmed in many Scriptures. "Yours, Lord, is the greatness and the power and the glory and the splendor and the majesty, for everything in the heavens and on earth belongs to You. Yours, Lord, is the kingdom, and You are exalted as head over all. Riches and honor come from You, and You are the ruler of everything. In Your hand are power and might, and it is in Your hand to make great and to give strength to all." (1 Chron 29:11,12). "Hallelujah! For the Lord our God, the Almighty, reigns!" (Revelation 19:6) note, "reigns" now, not "will do so in the millennium." "O Lord God of our fathers, are not You God in heaven? and do You not rule over all the kingdoms of the nations? Power and might are in Your hand, and no one [not even the Devil himself] can stand against You." (2 Chron 20:6). Before Him presidents and popes, kings and emperors, are less than grasshoppers.

"But he stands alone, and who can oppose him? He does whatever He pleases" (Job 23:13). Ah, my reader, the God of Scripture is no make-believe monarch, no mere imaginary sovereign, but King of kings, and Lord of lords. "I know that You can do anything and no plan of Yours can be thwarted." (Job 42:2); or, as another has translated it, "no purpose of Your can be frustrated." All that He has designed He does. All that He has decreed He performs. "Our God is in heaven and does whatever He pleases." (Psalm

115:3); and why has He? Because "there is no wisdom nor understanding nor counsel against the Lord" (Pro 21:30).

God's supremacy over the works of His hands is vividly depicted in Scripture. Inanimate matter, irrational creatures, all perform their Maker's bidding. At His pleasure the Red Sea divided and its waters stood up as walls (Exo 14); the earth opened her mouth, and guilty rebels went down alive into the pit (Num 16). When He so ordered, the sun stood still (Josh 10); and on another occasion went backward ten degrees on the dial of Ahaz (Isa 38:8). To exemplify His supremacy, He made ravens carry food to Elijah (I Kings 17), iron to swim on top of the waters (2 Kings 6:5), lions to be tame when Daniel was cast into their den, fire to burn not when the three Hebrews were flung into its flames. Thus "the Lord does whatever He pleases in heaven and on earth, in the seas and all the depths." (Psalm 135:6).

God's supremacy is also demonstrated in His perfect rule over the wills of men. Let the reader ponder carefully Exodus 34:24. Three times in the year all the males of Israel were required to leave their homes and go up to Jerusalem. They lived in the midst of hostile people, who hated them for having appropriated their lands. What then, was to hinder the Canaanites from seizing their opportunity, and during the absence of the men, slaying the women and children and taking possession of their farms? If the hand of the Almighty was not upon the wills even of wicked men, how could He make this promise beforehand, that none should so much as "desire" their lands? Ah, "The king's heart is in the hand of the Lord; He directs it like a watercourse wherever He pleases" (Pro 21:1).

But, it may be objected, do we not read again and again in Scripture how that men defied God, resisted His will, broke His commandments, disregarded His warnings, and turned a deaf ear to all His exhortations? Certainly we do. And does this nullify all that we have said above? If it does, then the Bible plainly contradicts itself. But that cannot be. What the objector refers to, is simply the wickedness of man against the external Word of God; whereas what we have mentioned above is what God has purposed in Himself. The rule of conduct He has given us to walk by, is perfectly fulfilled by none of us; His own eternal "counsels" are accomplished to their minutest details.

The absolute and universal supremacy of God is affirmed with equal plainness and positiveness in the New Testament. There we are told that God "works all things after the counsel of His own will" (Eph 1:11)—the Greek for "works" means "to work effectually." For this reason we read, "For of Him, and through Him, and to Him, are all things: to whom be glory forever. Amen" (Rom 11:36). Men may boast that they are free agents, with a will of their own, and are at liberty to do as they please, but Scripture says to those who boast "we will go into such a city, and continue there a year, and buy and sell ... You ought to say, If the Lord will" (James 4:13,15)!

Here then is a sure resting-place for the heart. Our lives are neither the product of blind fate nor the result of capricious chance. Every detail of them was ordained from all eternity, and is now ordered by the living and reigning God. Not a hair of our heads can be touched without His permission. "A man's heart devises his way: but the Lord directs his steps" (Pro 16:9). What assurance, what strength, what comfort this should give the real Christian! "My times are in Your hand" (Psalm 31:15). Then let me "Rest in the Lord, and wait patiently for Him" (Psalm 37:7).

CHAPTER 6
The Sovereignty of God

The sovereignty of God may be defined as the exercise of His supremacy—see preceding chapter. Being infinitely elevated above the highest creature, He is the Most High, Lord of heaven and earth. Subject to none, influenced by none, absolutely independent; God does as He pleases, only as He pleases, always as He pleases. None can thwart Him, none can hinder Him. So His own Word expressly declares: "My counsel shall stand, and I will do all My pleasure" (Isa 46:10); "All the peoples of the earth are regarded as nothing. He does as He pleases with the powers of heaven and the peoples of the earth. No one can hold back His hand or say to Him—What have you done?" (Dan 4:35). Divine sovereignty means that God is God in fact, as well as in name, that He is on the Throne of the universe, directing all things, working all things "after the counsel of His own will" (Eph 1:11).

Rightly did the late Charles Haddon Spurgeon say in his sermon on Matthew 20-15—"There is no attribute more comforting to His children than that of God's sovereignty. Under the most adverse circumstances, in the most severe trials, they believe that sovereignty has ordained their afflictions, that sovereignty overrules them, and that sovereignty will sanctify them all. There is nothing for which the children ought more earnestly to contend than the doctrine of their Master over all creation—the kingship of God over all the works of His own hands—the throne of God and His right to sit upon that throne.

"On the other hand, there is no doctrine more hated by worldlings, no truth of which they have made such a football, as the great, stupendous, but yet most certain doctrine of the sovereignty of the infinite Jehovah. Men will allow God to be everywhere except on His throne. They will allow Him to be in His workshop to fashion worlds and make stars. They will allow Him to be in His almonry to dispense His alms and bestow His bounties. They will allow Him to sustain the earth and bear up the pillars thereof, or light the lamps of heaven, or rule the waves of the ever-moving ocean; but when God ascends His throne, His creatures then gnash their teeth!

"And we proclaim an enthroned God, and His right to do as He wills with His own, to dispose of His creatures as He thinks well, without consulting them in the matter; then it is that we are hissed and execrated, and then it is that men turn a deaf ear to us, for God on His throne—is not the God they love. But it is God upon the throne that we love to preach. It is God upon His throne whom we trust."

"Our God is in heaven and does whatever He pleases." Psalm 115:3. "I know that You can do anything, and no plan of Yours can be thwarted." Job 42:2. "The Lord does whatever He pleases in heaven and on earth, in the seas and all the depths." Psalm 135:6. Yes, dear reader, such is the imperial Potentate revealed in Holy Writ. Unrivaled in majesty, unlimited in power, unaffected by anything outside Himself. But we are living in a day when even the most "orthodox" seem afraid to admit the proper Godhood of God. They say that to press the sovereignty of God excludes human responsibility; whereas human responsibility is based upon divine sovereignty, and is the product of it.

God sovereignly chose to place each of His creatures on that particular footing which seemed good in His sight. He created angels: some He placed on a conditional footing, others He gave an immutable standing before Him (1 Tim 5:21), making Christ their head (Col 2:10). Let it not be overlooked that the angels which sinned (2 Peter 2:4), were as much His creatures as the angels that sinned not. Yet God foresaw they would fall, nevertheless He placed them on a mutable, creature, conditional footing, and allowed them to fall, though He was not the Author of their sin.

So too, God sovereignly placed Adam in the garden of Eden upon a conditional footing. Had He so pleased, He could have placed him upon an unconditional footing. He could have placed him on a footing as firm as that occupied by the unfallen angels. He could have placed him upon a footing as sure and as immutable as that which His saints have in Christ. But, instead, He chose to set him in Eden on the basis of creature responsibility, so that he stood or fell according as he measured up or failed to measure up to his responsibility—obedience to his Maker. Adam stood accountable to God by the law which his Creator had given him. Here was responsibility, unimpaired responsibility, tested out under the most favorable conditions.

Now God did not place Adam upon a footing of conditional, creature responsibility, because it was right He should so place him? No, it was right because God did it. God did not even give creatures being because it was right for Him to do so, that is, because He was under any obligations to create; but it was right because He did so. God is sovereign. His will is supreme. So far from God being under any law of "right," He is a law unto Himself, so that whatever He does is right. And woe be to the rebel that calls His sovereignty into question: "Woe to him who quarrels with his Maker, to him who is but a potsherd among the potsherds on the ground. Does the clay say to the potter, 'What are you making?' Does your work say, 'He has no hands'?" (Isa 45:9).

Again; the Lord God sovereignly placed Israel upon a conditional footing. The 19th, 20th and 24th chapters of Exodus afford a clear and full proof of this. They were placed under a covenant of works. God gave to them certain laws, and made national blessing for them depend upon their observance of His statutes. But Israel was stiff-necked and uncircumcised in heart. They rebelled against Jehovah, forsook His law, turned unto false gods, and apostatized. In consequence, divine judgment fell upon them, they were delivered into the hands of their enemies, dispersed abroad throughout the earth, and remain under the heavy frown of God's displeasure to this day.

It was God in the exercise of His high sovereignty which placed Satan and his angels, Adam, and Israel in their respective responsible positions. But so far from His sovereignty taking away responsibility from the creature, it was by the exercise thereof that He placed them on this conditional footing, under such responsibilities as He thought proper; by virtue of which sovereignty, He is seen to be God over all. Thus, there is perfect harmony between the sovereignty of God and the responsibility of the creature. Many have most foolishly said that it is quite impossible to show where divine sovereignty ends and creature accountability begins. Here is where creature responsibility begins—in the sovereign ordination of the Creator. As to His sovereignty, there is not and never will be any "end" to it!

Let us give further proofs that the responsibility of the creature is based upon God's sovereignty. How many things are recorded in Scripture which were right because God commanded them, and which would not have been right had He not so commanded! What right had Adam to "eat" of the trees of the Garden? The permission of his Maker (Gen 2:16), without which he would have been a thief! What right had Israel to "borrow" of the Egyptians' jewels and clothing (Exo 12:35)? None, unless Jehovah had authorized it (Exo 3:22). What right had Israel to slay so many lambs for sacrifice? None, except that God commanded it. What right had Israel to kill off all the Canaanites? None, but as Jehovah had bidden them. What right has the husband to require submission from his wife? None, unless God had appointed it. And so we might go on. Human responsibility is based upon divine sovereignty.

One more example of the exercise of God's absolute sovereignty. God placed His elect upon a different footing from Adam or Israel. He placed His elect upon an unconditional footing. In the Everlasting Covenant Jesus Christ was appointed their Head, took their responsibilities upon Himself, and wrought out a righteousness for them which is perfect, indefeasible, and eternal. Christ was placed upon a conditional footing, for He was "made under the law, to redeem them that were under the law," only with this infinite difference; the others failed; He did not and could not. And who placed Christ upon that conditional footing? The Triune God. It was sovereign will which appointed Him, sovereign love which sent Him, sovereign authority which assigned Him His work.

Certain conditions were set before the Mediator. He was to be made in the likeness of sin's flesh; He was to magnify the law and make it honorable; He was to bear all the sins of all God's people in His own body on the tree; He was to make full atonement for them; He was to endure the outpoured wrath of God; He was to die and be buried. On the fulfillment of those conditions, He was promised a reward: Isaiah 53:10-12. He was to be the Firstborn among many brethren; He was to have a people who should share His glory. Blessed be His name forever, He fulfilled those conditions, and because He did so, the Father stands pledged, on solemn oath, to preserve through time and bless throughout eternity, everyone of those for whom His incarnate Son mediated. Because He took their place, they now share His. His righteousness is theirs, His standing before God is theirs, His life is theirs. There is not a single condition for them to meet, not a single responsibility for them to discharge in order to attain their eternal bliss. "By one offering He has perfected forever them that are sanctified [set apart]" (Heb 10:14).

Here then is the sovereignty of God openly displayed before all, displayed in the different ways in which He has dealt with His creatures. Part of the angels, Adam, and Israel, were placed upon a conditional footing, continuance in blessing being made dependent upon their obedience and fidelity to God. But in sharp contrast from them, the "little flock" (Luke 12:32), have been given an unconditional, an immutable standing in God's covenant, God's counsels, God's Son; their blessing being made dependent upon what Christ did for them. The foundation of God stands sure, having this seal, The Lord knows those who are His" (2 Tim 2:19). The foundation on which God's elect stand is a perfect one: nothing can be added to it, nor anything taken from it (Eccl 3:14). Here, then, is the highest and grandest display of the absolute sovereignty of God. Truly, He has "mercy on whom He will have mercy, and whom He will He hardens" (Rom 9:18).

CHAPTER 7
The Immutability of God

Immutability is one of the divine perfections which is not sufficiently pondered. It is one of the excellencies of the Creator which distinguishes Him from all His creatures. God is perpetually the same: subject to no change in His being, attributes, or determinations. Therefore God is compared to a "Rock" (Deut 32:4, etc.) which remains immovable, when the entire ocean surrounding it is continually in a fluctuating state; even so, though all creatures are subject to change, God is immutable. Because God has no beginning and no ending, He can know no change. He is everlastingly "the Father of lights, with whom is no variableness, neither shadow of turning" (James 1:17).

First, God is immutable in His essence. His nature and being are infinite, and so, subject to no mutations. There never was a time when He was not; there never will come a time when He shall cease to be. God has neither evolved, grown, nor improved. All that He is today, He has ever been, and ever will be. "I am the Lord, I do not change" (Mal 3:6) is His own unqualified affirmation. He cannot change for the better, for He is already perfect; and being perfect, He cannot change for the worse. Altogether unaffected by anything outside Himself, improvement or deterioration is impossible. He is perpetually the same. He only can say, "I AM THAT I AM" (Exo 3:14). He is altogether uninfluenced by the flight of time. There is no wrinkle upon the brow of eternity. Therefore His power can never diminish nor His glory ever fade.

Secondly, God is immutable in His attributes. Whatever the attributes of God were before the universe was called into existence, they are precisely the same now, and will remain so forever. Necessarily so; for they are the very perfections, the essential qualities of His being. Semper idem (always the same) is written across everyone of them. His power is unabated, His wisdom undiminished, His holiness unsullied. The attributes of God can no more change than Deity can cease to be. His veracity is immutable, for His Word is "forever ... settled in heaven" (Psalm 119:89). His love is eternal: "I have loved you with an everlasting love" (Jer 31:3) and "Having loved His own which were in the world, He loved them unto the end" (John 13:1). His mercy ceases not, for it is "everlasting" (Psalm 100:5).

Thirdly, God is immutable in His counsel. His will never varies. Perhaps some are ready to object that we ought to read the following: "And it repented the Lord that He had made man" (Gen 6:6). Our first reply is, Then do the Scriptures contradict themselves? No, that cannot be. Numbers 23:19 is plain enough: "God is not a man, that He should lie; neither the son of man, that He should repent." So also in I Samuel 15:29, "The Strength of Israel will not lie nor repent: for He is not a man, that He should repent." The explanation is very simple. When speaking of Himself, God frequently accommodates His language to our limited capacities. He describes Himself as clothed with bodily members, as eyes, ears, hands, etc. He speaks of Himself as "waking" (Psalm 78:65), as "rising up early" (Jer 7:13); yet He neither slumbers nor sleeps. When He institutes a change in His dealings with men, He describes His course of conduct as "repenting.

Yes, God is immutable in His counsel. "The gifts and calling of God are without repentance" (Rom 11:29). It must be so, for "He is in one mind, and who can turn from Him? and what His soul desires, even that He does" (Job 23:13). "Change and decay in all around we see, May He who changes not abide with thee."

God's purpose never alters. One of two things causes a man to change his mind and reverse his plans: lack of foresight to anticipate everything, or lack of power to execute them. But as God is both omniscient and omnipotent there is never any need for Him to revise His decrees. No, "the plans of the Lord stand firm forever, the purposes of His heart through all generations" (Psalm 33:11). Therefore do we read of "His unchangeable purpose" (Heb 6:17).

Herein we may perceive the infinite distance which separates the highest creature from the Creator. Creaturehood and mutability are correlative terms. If the creature was not mutable by nature it would not be a creature; it would be God. By nature we tend toward nothingness, since we came from nothing. Nothing stops our annihilation but the will and sustaining power of God. None can sustain himself a single moment. We are entirely dependent on the Creator for every breath we draw. We gladly own with the Psalmist, You "holds our soul in life" (Psalm 66:9). The realization of this ought to make us lie down under a sense of our own nothingness in the presence of Him in

Whom "we live, and move, and have our being" (Acts 17:28).

As fallen creatures we are not only mutable, but everything in us is opposed to God. As such we are "wandering stars" (Jude 13), out of our proper orbit. "The wicked are like the troubled sea, when it cannot rest" (Isa 57:20). Fallen man is inconstant. The words of Jacob concerning Reuben apply with full force to all of Adam's descendants: "unstable as water" (Gen 49:4). Thus it is not only a mark of piety, but also the part of wisdom to heed that injunction, "cease from man" (Isa 2:22). No human being is to be depended on. "Do not put your trust in princes, in mortal men, who cannot save" (Psalm 146:3). If I disobey God, then I deserve to be deceived and disappointed by my fellows. People who like you today, may hate you tomorrow. The multitude who cried, "Hosanna to the Son of David!" speedily changed to "Away with Him, crucify Him!"

Herein is solid comfort. Human nature cannot be relied upon; but God can! However unstable I may be, however fickle my friends may prove, God changes not. If He varied as we do; if He willed one thing today and another tomorrow; if He were controlled by caprice, who could confide in Him? But, all praise to His glorious name, He is ever the same. His purpose is fixed; His will is stable; His word is sure. Here then is a Rock on which we may fix our feet, while the mighty torrent is sweeping away everything around us. The permanence of God's character guarantees the fulfillment of His promises: "For the mountains shall depart, and the hills be removed; but My kindness shall not depart from you, neither shall the covenant of My peace be removed, says the Lord who has mercy on you" (Isa 54:10).

Herein is encouragement to prayer. "What comfort would it be to pray to a God that, like the chameleon, changed color every moment? Who would put up a petition to an earthly prince that was so mutable as to grant a petition one day, and deny it another?" (Stephen Charnock, 1670).

Should someone ask, But what is the use of praying to One whose will is already fixed? We answer, Because He so requires it. What blessings has God promised without our seeking them? "If we ask anything according to His will, He hears us" (1 John 5:14), and He has willed everything that is for His child's good. To ask for anything contrary to His will is not prayer, but rank rebellion.

Herein is terror for the wicked. Those who defy Him, who break His laws, who have no concern for His glory, but who live their lives as though He existed not, must not suppose that, when at the last they shall cry to Him for mercy, He will alter His will, revoke His word, and rescind His awful threatenings. No, He has declared, "Therefore will I also deal in fury: My eye shall not spare, neither will I have pity: and though they cry in My ears with a loud voice, yet will I not hear them" (Eze 8:18). God will not deny Himself to gratify their lusts. God is holy, unchangingly so. Therefore God hates sin, eternally hates it. Hence the eternality of the punishment of all who die in their sins.

"The divine immutability, like the cloud which interposed between the Israelites and the Egyptian army, has a dark as well as a light side. It insures the execution of His threatenings, as well as the performance of His promises; and destroys the hope which the guilty fondly cherish, that He will be all lenity to His frail and erring creatures, and that they will be much more lightly dealt with than the declarations of His own Word would lead us to expect. We oppose to these deceitful and presumptuous speculations the solemn truth—that God is unchanging in veracity and purpose, in faithfulness and justice" (John Dick, 1850).

CHAPTER 8
The Holiness of God

"Who shall not fear You, O Lord, and glorify Your name? for You alone are holy" (Rev 15:4). God only is independently, infinitely, immutably holy. In Scripture He is frequently styled "The Holy ONE": He is so because the sum of all moral excellency is found in Him. He is absolute Purity, unsullied even by the shadow of sin. "God is light, and in Him is no darkness at all" (1 John 1:5). Holiness is the very excellency of the divine nature: the great God is "glorious in holiness" (Exo 15:11). Therefore do we read, "You are of purer eyes than to behold evil, and can not look on iniquity" (Hab 1:13). As God's power is the opposite of the native weakness of the creature; as His wisdom is in complete contrast from the least defect of understanding or folly; so His holiness is the very antithesis of all moral blemish or defilement. Of old God appointed singers in Israel "that should praise the beauty of holiness" (2 Chron 20:21). "Power is God's hand or arm; omniscience His eye; mercy, His heart; eternity His duration, but holiness is His beauty" (S. Charnock). It is this, supremely, which renders Him lovely to those who are delivered from sin's dominion. A chief emphasis is placed upon this perfection of God:

"God is more often styled Holy than Almighty, and set forth by this part of His dignity more than by any other. This is more fixed on as an epithet to His name than any other. You never find it expressed 'His mighty name' or 'His wise name' but His great name, and most of all, His holy name. This is the greatest title of honor; in this latter does the majesty and venerableness of His name appear" (S. Charnock).

This perfection, as none other, is solemnly celebrated before the Throne of Heaven, the seraphim crying, "Holy, holy, holy, is the Lord of hosts" (Isa 6:3). God Himself singles out this perfection, "Once have I sworn by My holiness" (Psalm 89:35). God swears by His "holiness" because that is a fuller expression of Himself than anything else. Therefore we are exhorted, "Sing unto the Lord, O saints of His, and give thanks at the remembrance of His holiness" (Psalm 30:4). "Holiness may be said to be a transcendental attribute, that, as it were, runs through the rest, and casts luster upon them. It is an attribute of attributes" (J. Howe, 1670). Thus we read: "the beauty of the Lord" (Psalm 27:4), which is none other than "the beauty of holiness" (Psalm 110:3).

"As holiness seems to claim an excellency above all His other perfections, so it is the glory of all the rest: as it is the glory of the Godhead, so it is the glory of every perfection in the Godhead; as His power is the strength of them, so His holiness is the beauty of them; as all would be weak without almightiness to back them, so all would be uncommonly without holiness to adorn them. Should this be sullied, all the rest would lose their honor; as at the same instant the sun should lose its light, it would lose its heat, its strength, its generative and quickening virtue. As sincerity is the luster of every grace in a Christian, so is purity the splendor of every attribute in the Godhead. His justice is a holy justice, His wisdom a holy wisdom, His power a 'holy arm' (Psalm 98:1). His truth or promise a 'holy promise' (Psalm 105:42). His name, which signifies all His attributes in conjunction is 'holy'" (Psalm 103:1) (S. Charnock).

God's holiness is manifested in His works. "The Lord is righteous in all His ways, and holy in all His works" (Psalm 145:17). Nothing but that which is excellent can proceed from Him. Holiness is the rule of all His actions. At the beginning He pronounced all that He made "very good" (Gen 1:31), which He could not have done had there been anything imperfect or unholy in them. Man was made "upright" (Eccl 7:29), in the image and likeness of his Creator. The angels that fell were created holy, for we are told that they "kept not their first habitation" (Jude 6). Of Satan it is written, "You were perfect in your ways from the day that the were created, until iniquity was found in you" (Eze 28:15).

God's holiness is manifested in His law. That law forbids sin in all of its modifications: in its most refined as well as its grossest forms, the intent of the mind as well as the pollution of the body, the secret desire as well as the overt act. Therefore do we read, "The law is holy, and the commandment holy, and just, and good" (Rom 7:12). Yes, "the commandment of the Lord is pure, enlightening the eyes. The fear of the Lord is clean, enduring forever: the judgments of the Lord are true and righteous altogether" (Psalm 19:8,9).

God's holiness is best manifested at the cross. Wondrously and yet most solemnly does the atonement display God's infinite holiness and abhorrence of sin. How hateful sin must be to God for Him to punish it to its utmost deserts when it was imputed to His Son!

"Not all the vials of judgment that have or shall be poured out upon the wicked world, nor the flaming furnace of a sinner's conscience, nor the irreversible sentence pronounced against the rebellious demons, nor the groans of the damned creatures, give such a demonstration of God's hatred of sin, as the wrath of God let loose upon His Son! Never did divine holiness appear more beautiful and lovely than at the time our Savior's countenance was most marred in the midst of His dying groans. This He Himself acknowledges in Psalm 22. When God had turned His smiling face from Him, and thrust His sharp knife into His heart, which forced that terrible cry from Him, 'My God, My God, why have You forsaken Me?' He adores this perfection—'You are holy'" (v.3) (S. Charnock).

Because God is holy He hates all sin. He loves everything which is in conformity to His laws, and loathes everything which is contrary to it. His Word plainly declares, "wicked people are an abomination to the Lord" (Prov 3:32). And again, "The thoughts of the wicked are an abomination to the Lord" (Prov 15:26). It follows, therefore, that He must necessarily punish sin. Sin can no more exist without demanding His punishment than without requiring His hatred of it. God has often forgiven sinners, but He never forgives sin; and the sinner is only forgiven on the ground of Another having born his punishment: for "without shedding of blood is no remission" (Heb 9:22). Therefore we are told "The Lord will take vengeance on His adversaries, and He reserves wrath for His enemies" (Nahum 1:2). For one sin God banished our first parents from Eden. For one sin all the posterity of Canaan, fell under a curse which remains over them to this day (Gen 9:21). For one sin Moses was excluded from Canaan. For one sin Elisha's servant smitten with leprosy. For one sin Ananias and Sapphira were cut off out of the land of the living.

Herein we find proof for the divine inspiration of the Scriptures. The unregenerate do not really believe in the holiness of God. Their conception of His character is altogether one-sided. They fondly hope that His mercy will override everything else. "You thought that I was just like you" (Psalm 50:21) is God's charge against them. They think only of a "God" patterned after their own evil hearts. Hence their continuance in a course of mad folly. Such is the holiness ascribed to the divine nature and character in the Scriptures, that it clearly demonstrates their superhuman origin. The character attributed to the "gods" of the ancients and of modern heathendom is the very reverse of that immaculate purity which pertains to the true God. An ineffably holy God, who has the utmost abhorrence of all sin, was never invented by any of Adam's fallen descendants! The fact is, that nothing makes more manifest the terrible depravity of man's heart and his enmity against the living God, than to have set before him One who is infinitely and immutably holy. His own idea of sin is practically limited to what the world calls "crime." Anything short of that, man palliates as "defects," "mistakes," "infirmities," etc. And even where sin is owned at all, excuses and extenuations are made for it.

The god which the vast majority of professing Christians "love" is looked upon very much like an indulgent old man, who himself has no relish for folly, but leniently winks at the "indiscretions" of youth. But the Word says, "You hate all workers of iniquity" (Psalm 5:5). And again, "God is angry with the wicked every day" (Psalm 7:11). But men refuse to believe in this God, and gnash their teeth when His hatred of sin is faithfully pressed upon their attention. No, sinful man was no more likely to devise a holy God than to create the Lake of Fire in which he will be tormented forever and ever!

Because God is holy, acceptance with Him on the ground of creature doings is utterly impossible. A fallen creature could sooner create a world than produce that which would meet the approval of infinite Purity. Can darkness dwell with Light? Can the Immaculate One take pleasure in "filthy rags" (Isa 64:6)? The best that sinful man brings forth is defiled. A corrupt tree cannot bear good fruit. God would deny Himself, vilify His perfections, were He to account as righteous and holy that which is not so in itself; and nothing is so which has the least stain upon it contrary to the nature of God. But blessed be His name, that which His holiness demanded, His grace has provided in Christ Jesus our Lord. Every poor sinner who has fled to Him for refuge stands "accepted in the Beloved" (Eph 1:6). Hallelujah!

Because God is holy the utmost reverence becomes our approaches unto Him. "God is greatly to be feared in the assembly of the saints, and to be had in reverence of all those who are about Him" (Psalm 89:7). Then "Exalt the Lord our God, and worship at His footstool; He is holy" (Psalm 99:5). Yes, "at His footstool," in the lowest posture of humility, prostrate before Him. When Moses would approach unto the burning bush, God said, "Take off your shoes from off your feet" (Exo 3:5). He is to be served "with fear" (Psalm 2:11). Of Israel His demand was, "I will show Myself holy among those who are near me. I will be glorified before all the people." (Lev 10:3).

The more our hearts are awed by His ineffable holiness, the more acceptable will be our approaches unto Him.

Because God is holy we should desire to be conformed to Him. His commandment is, "Be holy, for I am holy" (1 Peter 1:16). We are not bidden to be omnipotent or omniscient as God is, but "as the One who called you is holy, you also are to be holy in all your conduct" (1 Peter 1:15).

"This is the prime way of honoring God. We do not so glorify God by elevated admirations, or eloquent expressions, or pompous services for Him, as when we aspire to a conversing with Him with unstained spirits, and live to Him in living like Him" (S. Charnock).

Then as God alone is the Source and Fount of holiness, let us earnestly seek holiness from Him; let our daily prayer be that He may "sanctify us wholly; and our whole spirit and soul and body be preserved blameless unto the coming of our Lord Jesus Christ" (1 Thess 5:23).

CHAPTER 9
The Power of God

We cannot have a right conception of God unless we think of Him as all-powerful, as well as all-wise. He who cannot do what he will, and perform all his pleasure, cannot be God. As God has a will to resolve what He deems good, so has He power to execute His will.

"The power of God is that ability and strength whereby He can bring to pass whatever He pleases, whatever His infinite wisdom may direct, and whatever the infinite purity of His will may resolve ... As holiness is the beauty of all God's attributes, so power is that which gives life and action to all the perfections of the divine nature. How vain would be the eternal counsels, if power did not step in to execute them. Without power—His mercy would be but feeble pity, His promises an empty sound, His threatenings a mere scarecrow. God's power is like Himself—infinite, eternal, incomprehensible; it can neither be checked, restrained, nor frustrated by the creature" (Stephen Charnock).

"God has spoken once; twice have I heard this, that power belongs unto God" (Psalm 62:11). "God has spoken once": nothing more is necessary! Heaven and earth shall pass away, but His word abides forever." "God has spoken once": how befitting His divine majesty! We poor mortals may speak often and yet fail to be heard. He speaks but once and the thunder of His power is heard on a thousand hills.

"The Lord thundered from heaven; the voice of the Most High resounded. He shot his arrows and scattered the enemies, great bolts of lightning and routed them. The valleys of the sea were exposed and the foundations of the earth laid bare at your rebuke, O Lord, at the blast of breath from your nostrils." (Psalm 18:13-15).

"God has spoken once": behold His unchanging authority. "For who in the heaven can be compared unto the Lord? who among the sons of the mighty can be likened unto the Lord?" (Psalm 89:6). "All the peoples of the earth are regarded as nothing. He does as He pleases with the powers of heaven and the peoples of the earth. No one can hold back His hand or say to Him—

What have You done?" (Dan 4:35). This was openly displayed when God became incarnate and tabernacled among men. To the leper He said, "I will; be clean. And immediately his leprosy was cleansed' (Matt 8:3). To one who had lain in the grave four days He cried, "Lazarus, come forth," and the dead came forth. The stormy wind and the angry waves were hushed at a single word from Him. A legion of demons could not resist His authoritative command.

"Power belongs unto God," and to Him alone. Not a creature in the entire universe has an atom of power—but what God delegates. But God's power is not acquired, nor does it depend upon any recognition by any other authority. It belongs to Him inherently.

"God's power is like Himself, self-existent, self-sustained. The mightiest of men cannot add so much as a shadow of increased power to the Omnipotent One. He sits on no buttressed throne and leans on no assisting arm. His court is not maintained by His courtiers, not does it borrow its splendor from His creatures. He is Himself the great central source and Originator of all power" (C. H. Spurgeon).

Not only does all creation bear witness to the great power of God, but also to His entire independency of all created things. Listen to His own challenge: ""Where were you when I laid the earth's foundation? Tell me, if you understand. Who marked off its dimensions? Surely you know! Who stretched a measuring line across it? On what were its footings set, or who laid its cornerstone?" (Job 38:4-6). How completely is the pride of man laid in the dust!

"Power is also used as a name of God, 'the Son of man sitting on the right hand of power' (Mark 14:62), that is, at the right hand of God. God and power are so inseparable that they are reciprocated. As His essence is immense, not to be confined in place; as it is eternal, not to be measured in time; so it is almighty, not to be limited in regard of action" (S. Charnock).

"Lo, these are parts of His ways: but how little a portion is heard of Him? but the thunder of His power who can understand?" (Job 26:14). Who is able to count all the monuments of His power? Even that which is displayed of His might in the visible creation is utterly beyond our powers of comprehension, still less are we able to conceive of omnipotence itself. There is infinitely more power lodged in the nature of God than is expressed in all His works.

"Parts of His ways" we behold in creation, providence, redemption, but only a "little part" of His might is seen in them. Remarkably is this brought out—"And there was the hiding of His power" (Hab 3:4). It is scarcely possible to imagine anything more grandiose than the imagery of this whole chapter, yet nothing in it surpasses the nobility of this statement. The prophet (in vision) beheld the mighty God scattering the hills and overturning the mountains, which one would think afforded an amazing demonstration of His power. Nay, says our verse, that is rather the "hiding" than the displaying of His power. What is meant? This: so inconceivable, so immense, so uncontrollable is the power of Deity, that the fearful convulsions which He works in nature conceal, more than they reveal, of His infinite might!

It is very beautiful to link together the following passages: He "treads upon the waves of the sea" (Job 9:8), which expresses God's uncontrollable power. "He walks in the circuit of Heaven" (Job 22:14), which tells of the immensity of His presence. He "walks upon the wings of the wind' (Psalm 104:3), which signifies the amazing swiftness of His operations. This last expression is very remarkable. It is not that He "flies," or "runs," but that He "walks" and that, on the very "wings of the wind"—on the most impetuous of the elements, tossed into utmost rage, and sweeping along with almost inconceivable rapidity, yet they are under His feet, beneath His perfect control!

Let us now consider God's power in creation. "The heavens are yours, and the earth is yours; everything in the world is yours—you created it all. You created north and south" (Psalm 89:11, 12). Before man can work he must have both tools and materials, but God began with nothing, and by His word alone out of nothing made all things. The intellect cannot grasp it. "God spoke, and it was done; He commanded, and it stood fast" (Psalm 33:9). Primeval matter heard His voice. "God said, Let there be ... and it was so" (Gen 1). Well may we exclaim, "Powerful is your arm! Strong is your hand! Your right hand is lifted high in glorious strength" (Psalm 89:13).

"Who, that looks upward to the midnight sky; and, with an eye of reason, beholds its rolling wonders; who can forbear enquiring, Of what were their mighty orbs formed? Amazing to relate, they were produced without materials. They sprung from emptiness itself. The stately fabric of universal nature emerged out of nothing. What instruments were used by the Supreme Architect to fashion the parts with such exquisite niceness, and give so beautiful a polish to the whole? How was it all connected into one finely-proportioned and nobly finished structure? A bare fiat accomplished all. 'Let them be', said God. He added no more; and at once the marvelous edifice arose, adorned with every beauty, displaying innumerable perfections, and declaring amidst enraptured seraphs its great Creator's praise. 'The Lord merely spoke, and the heavens were created. He breathed the word, and all the stars were born' (Psalm 33:6)" James Hervey, 1789).

Consider God's power in preservation. No creature has power to preserve itself. "Can papyrus reeds grow where there is no marsh? Can bulrushes flourish where there is no water?" (Job 8:11). Both man and beast would perish if there were not herbs for food; herbs would wither and die if the earth were not refreshed with fruitful showers. Therefore is God called the Preserver of "man and beast" (Psalm 36:6), "upholding all things by the word of His power" (Heb 1:3). What a marvel of divine power is the prenatal life of every human being! That an infant can live at all, and for so many months, in such cramped and filthy quarters, and that without breathing, is unaccountable without the power of God. Truly He "holds our soul in life" (Psalm 66:9).

The preservation of the earth from the violence of the sea is another plain instance of God's might. How is that raging element kept pent within those limits wherein He first lodged it, continuing its channel, without overflowing the earth and dashing in pieces the lower part of the creation? The natural situation of the water is to be above the earth, because it is lighter, and immediately under the air, because it is heavier. Who restrains the natural quality of it? Certainly man does not, and cannot. It is the fiat of its Creator which alone bridles it: "Hitherto shall you come, but no further: and here shall your proud waves be stayed" (Job 38:11). What a standing monument to the power of God is the preservation of the world!

Consider God's power in government. Take His restraining of the malice of Satan. "The devil, as a roaring lion, walks about, seeking whom he may devour" (1 Peter 5:8). He is filled with hatred against God, and with fiendish enmity against men, particularly the saints. He who envied Adam in paradise envies us the pleasure of enjoying any of God's blessings. Could he have his will, he would treat all the same way he treated Job: he would send fire from heaven on the fruits of the earth, destroy the cattle, cause a wind to overthrow our houses, and cover our bodies with boils. But, little as men may realize it, God bridles him to a large extent, prevents him from carrying out his evil designs, and confines him within His ordinations.

So too God restrains the natural corruption of men. He allows sufficient outbreakings of sin to show what fearful havoc has been wrought by man's apostasy from his Maker, but who can conceive the frightful lengths to which men would go were God to remove His curbing hand? "Whose mouth is full of cursing and bitterness, their feet are swift to shed blood" (Rom 3:14,15). This is the nature of every descendant of Adam. Then what unbridled licentiousness and headstrong folly would triumph in the world, if the power of God did not interpose to lock down the floodgates of it! See Psalm 93:3, 4.

Consider God's power in judgment. When He smites, none can resist Him: see Ezekiel 22:14. How terribly this was exemplified at the Flood! God opened the windows of heaven and broke up the great fountains of the deep, and (excepting those in the ark) the entire human race, helpless before the storm of His wrath, was swept away. A shower of fire and brimstone from heaven, and the cities of the plain were exterminated. Pharaoh and all his armies were impotent when God blew upon them at the Red Sea. What a terrific word is that in Romans 9:22: "What if God, willing to show His wrath, and to make His power known, endured with much longsuffering the vessels of wrath fitted to destruction." God is going to display His mighty power upon the reprobate not merely by incarcerating them in Gehenna, but by supernaturally preserving their bodies as well as souls amid the eternal burnings of the Lake of Fire. Well may all tremble before such a God! To treat with impudence One who can crush us more easily than we can a moth, is a suicidal policy. To openly defy Him who is clothed with omnipotence, who can rend us in pieces or cast us into Hell any moment He pleases, is the very height of insanity. To put it on its lowest ground, it is but the part of wisdom to heed His command, "Kiss the Son, lest he be angry and you be destroyed in your way, for his wrath can flare up in a moment. Blessed are all who take refuge in him." (Psalm 2:12).

Well may the enlightened soul adore such a God! The wondrous and infinite perfections of such a Being call for fervent worship. If men of might and renown claim the admiration of the world, how much more should the power of the Almighty fill us with wonderment and homage. "Who among the gods is like you, O Lord? Who is like you--majestic in holiness, awesome in glory, working wonders?" (Exo 15:11).

Well may the saint trust such a God! He is worthy of implicit confidence. Nothing is too hard for Him. If God were stinted in might and had a limit to His strength we might well despair. But seeing that He is clothed with omnipotence, no prayer is too hard for Him to answer, no need too great for Him to supply, no passion too strong for Him to subdue; no temptation too powerful for Him to deliver from, no misery too deep for Him to relieve. "The Lord is my light and my salvation--whom shall I fear? The Lord is the stronghold of my life--of whom shall I be afraid?" (Psalm 27:1).

"Now to him who is able to do immeasurably more than all we ask or imagine, according to his power that is at work within us, to him be glory in the church and in Christ Jesus throughout all generations, for ever and ever! Amen." (Eph 3:20-21).

CHAPTER 10
The Faithfulness of God

Unfaithfulness is one of the most outstanding sins of these evil days. In the business world, a man's word is, with exceedingly rare exceptions, no longer his bond. In the social world, marital infidelity abounds on every hand, the sacred bonds of wedlock being broken with as little regard as the discarding of an old garment. In the ecclesiastical realm thousands who have solemnly covenanted to preach the truth make no scruple to attack and deny it. Nor can reader or writer claim complete immunity from this fearful sin. In how many ways have we been unfaithful to Christ, and to the light and privileges which God has entrusted to us! How refreshing, then, how unspeakably blessed, to lift our eyes above this scene of ruin, and behold One who is faithful—faithful in all things, faithful at all times.

"Know therefore that the Lord Your God, He is God, the faithful God" (Deut 7:9). This quality is essential to His being; without it He would not be God. For God to be unfaithful would be to act contrary to His nature, which is impossible: "If we believe not, yet He abides faithful; He cannot deny Himself" (2 Tim 2:13). Faithfulness is one of the glorious perfections of His being. He is as it were clothed with it: "O Lord God Almighty! Where is there anyone as mighty as you, Lord? Faithfulness is your very character" (Psalm 89:8). So too when God became incarnate it was said, "Righteousness will be his belt and faithfulness the sash around his waist" (Isa 11:5).

What a word is that in Psalm 36:5, "Your mercy, O Lord, is in the heavens; and Your faithfulness reaches unto the clouds." Far above all finite comprehension is the unchanging faithfulness of God. Everything about God is great, vast, incomparable. He never forgets, never fails, never falters, never forfeits His word. To every declaration of promise or prophecy the Lord has exactly adhered, every engagement of covenant or threatening He will make good, for "God is not a man, that he should lie, nor a son of man, that he should change his mind. Does he speak and then not act? Does he promise and not fulfill?" (Num 23:19). Therefore does the believer exclaim, "Because of the Lord's great love we are not consumed, for his compassions never fail. They are new every morning; great is your faithfulness" (Lam 3:22,23).

Scripture abounds in illustrations of God's faithfulness. More than four thousand years ago He said, "While the earth remains, seedtime and harvest, and cold and heat, and summer and winter, and day and night shall not cease" (Gen 8:22). Every year that comes furnishes a fresh witness to God's fulfillment of this promise. In Genesis 15 we find that Jehovah declared unto Abraham, "Your seed shall be a stranger in a land that is not theirs, and shall serve them ... But in the fourth generation they shall come hither again" (vv.13-16). Centuries ran their weary course. Abraham's descendants groaned amid the brick-kilns of Egypt. Had God forgotten His promise? No, indeed. Read Exodus 12:41, "At the end of the 430 years, to the very day, all the LORD's divisions left Egypt." Through Isaiah the Lord declared, "Behold, a virgin shall conceive, and bear a Son, and shall call His name Immanuel" (7:14). Again centuries passed, but "When the fullness of the time was come, God sent forth His Son, made of a woman" (Gal 4:4).

God is true. His Word of promise is sure. In all His relations with His people, God is faithful. He may be safely relied upon. No one ever yet really trusted Him in vain. We find this precious truth expressed almost everywhere in the Scriptures, for His people need to know that faithfulness is an essential part of the divine character. This is the basis of our confidence in Him. But it is one thing to accept the faithfulness of God as a divine truth, it is quite another to act upon it. God has given us many "exceeding great and precious promises," but are we really counting on His fulfillment of them? Are we actually expecting Him to do for us all that He has said? Are we resting with implicit assurance on these words, "He is faithful who promised" (Heb 10:23)?

There are seasons in the lives of all when it is not easy, no not even for Christians, to believe that God is faithful. Our faith is sorely tried, our eyes bedimmed with tears, and we can no longer trace the out-workings of His love. Our ears are distracted with the noises of the world, harassed by the atheistic whisperings of Satan, and we can no longer hear the sweet accents of His still small voice. Cherished plans have been thwarted, friends on whom we relied have failed us, a professed brother or sister in Christ has betrayed us. We are staggered. We sought to be faithful to God, and now a dark cloud hides Him from us. We find it difficult, yes, impossible, for carnal reason to harmonize His frowning providence with His gracious promises. Ah, faltering soul, severely tried fellow pilgrim, seek grace to heed Isaiah 50:10, "Who among you fears the Lord and obeys the word of his servant? Let him who walks in the dark, who has no light, trust in the name of the Lord and rely on his God."

When you are tempted to doubt the faithfulness of God, cry out, "Get you hence, Satan." Though you cannot now harmonize God's mysterious dealings with the avowals of His love, wait on Him for more light. In His own good time He will make it plain to you. "You do not realize now what I am doing, but later you will understand" (John 13:7). The sequel will yet demonstrate that God has neither forsaken nor deceived His child. "Yet the Lord longs to be gracious to you; he rises to show you compassion. For the Lord is a God of justice. Blessed are all who wait for him!" (Isa 30:18).

"Judge not the Lord by feeble sense,
But trust Him for His grace,
Behind a frowning providence
He hides a smiling face.
You fearful saints, fresh courage take,
The clouds you so much dread,
Are rich with mercy, and shall break
In blessing o'er your head."

"The statutes you have laid down are righteous; they are fully trustworthy" (Psalm 119:138). God has not only told us the best, but also He has told us the worst. He has faithfully described the ruin which the Fall has effected. He has faithfully diagnosed the terrible state which sin has produced. He has faithfully made known his inveterate hatred of evil, and that He must punish the same. He has faithfully warned us that He is "a consuming fire" (Heb 12:29). Not only does His Word abound in illustrations of His fidelity in fulfilling His promises, but it also records numerous examples of His faithfulness in making good His threatenings. Every stage of Israel's history exemplifies that solemn fact. So it was with individuals: Pharaoh, Korah, Achan and a multitude of others are so many proofs. And thus it will be with you, my reader—unless you have fled or do flee to Christ for refuge, the everlasting burning of the Lake of Fire will be your sure and certain portion! God who threatens, is faithful.

God is faithful in preserving His people. "God is faithful, by Whom you were called unto the fellowship of His Son" (1 Cor 1:9). In the previous verse promise was made that God would confirm unto the end His own people. The Apostle's confidence in the absolute security of believers was founded not on the strength of their resolutions or ability to persevere, but on the veracity of Him who cannot lie. Since God has promised to His Son a certain people for His inheritance, to deliver them from sin and condemnation, and to make them participants of eternal life in glory, it is certain that He will not allow any of them to perish.

God is faithful in disciplining His people. He is faithful in what He withholds—no less than in what He gives. He is faithful in sending sorrow as well—as in giving joy. The faithfulness of God is a truth to be confessed by us not only when we are at ease—but also when we are smarting under the sharpest rebuke. Nor must this confession be merely of our mouths, but of our hearts, too. When God smites us with the rod of chastisement, it is faithfulness which wields it. To acknowledge this means that we humble ourselves before Him, own that we fully deserve His correction, and instead of murmuring, thank Him for it. God never afflicts without a reason. "For this cause many are weak and sickly among you" (1 Cor 11:30), says Paul, illustrating this principle. When His rod falls upon us let us say with Daniel, "O Lord, righteousness belongs unto You, but unto us confusion of faces" (9:7).

"I know, O Lord, that Your judgments are right, and that You in faithfulness have afflicted me" (Psalm 119:75). Trouble and affliction are not only consistent with God's love pledged in the everlasting covenant, but they are parts of the administration of the same. God is not only faithful notwithstanding afflictions, but faithful in sending them. "Then will I visit their transgression with the rod, and their iniquity with stripes. Nevertheless My loving-kindness will I not utterly take from him, nor allow My faithfulness to fail" (Psalm 89:32,33). Chastening is not only reconcilable with God's loving-kindness, but it is the effect and expression of it. It would much quiet the minds of God's people if they would remember that His covenant love binds Him to lay on them seasonable correction. Afflictions are necessary for us: "In their affliction they will seek Me early" (Hosea 5:15).

God is faithful in glorifying His people. "Faithful is He who calls you, Who also will do it" (1 Thess 5:24). The immediate reference here is to the saints being "preserved blameless unto the coming of our Lord Jesus Christ." God deals with us not on the ground of our merits (for we have none), but for His own great name's sake. God is constant to Himself and to His own purpose of grace: "whom He called ... them He also glorified" (Rom 8:30). God gives a full demonstration of the constancy of His everlasting goodness toward His elect by effectually calling them out of darkness into His marvelous light, and this should fully assure them of the certain continuance of it. "The foundation of God stands sure' (2 Tim 2:19). Paul was resting on the faithfulness of God when he said, "I know whom I have believed, and am persuaded that He is able to keep that which I have committed unto Him against that day" (2 Tim 1:12).

The apprehension of this blessed truth will preserve us from worry. To be full of care, to view our situation with dark forebodings, to anticipate the morrow with sad anxiety—is to reflect poorly upon the faithfulness of God. He who has cared for His child through all the years will not forsake him in old age. He who has heard your prayers in the past will not refuse to supply your need in the present emergency. Rest on Job 5:19, "He shall deliver you in six troubles: yes, in seven there shall no evil touch you."

The apprehension of this blessed truth will check our murmurings. The Lord knows what is best for each one of us, and one effect of resting on this truth will be the silencing of our petulant complainings. God is greatly honored when, under trial and chastening, we have good thoughts of Him, vindicate His wisdom and justice, and recognize His love in His very rebukes.

The apprehension of this blessed truth will beget increasing confidence in God. "Therefore let those who suffer according to the will of God commit the keeping of their souls to Him in well doing, as unto a faithful Creator" (1 Peter 4:19). When we trustfully resign ourselves, and all our affairs into God's hands, fully persuaded of His love and faithfulness, the sooner shall we be satisfied with His providences and realize that "He does all things well."

CHAPTER 11
The Goodness of God

"The goodness of God endures continually" (Psalm 52:1). The goodness of God refers to the perfection of His nature: "God is light, and in Him is no darkness at all" (1 John 1:5). There is such an absolute perfection in God's nature and being that nothing is lacking to it or defective in it, and nothing can be added to it to make it better.

"He is originally good, good of Himself, which nothing else is; for all creatures are good only by participation and communication from God. He is essentially good; not only good, but goodness itself: the creature's good is a superadded quality, in God it is His essence. He is infinitely good; the creature's good is but a drop, but in God there in an infinite ocean or gathering together of good. He is eternally and immutably good, for He cannot be less good than He is; as there can be no addition made to Him, so no subtraction from Him" (Thomas Manton). God is summum bonum—the highest good.

The original Saxon meaning of our English word God is "The Good." God is not only the greatest of all beings, but the best. All the goodness there is in any creature has been imparted from the Creator, but God's goodness is underived, for it is the essence of His eternal nature. As God is infinite in power from all eternity, before there was any display thereof, or any act of omnipotence put forth, so He was eternally good before there was any communication of His bounty, or any creature to whom it might be imparted. Thus, the first manifestation of this divine perfection was in giving being to all things. "You are good, and do good" (Psalm 119:68). God has in Himself an infinite and inexhaustible treasure of all blessedness, enough to fill all things.

All that emanates from God—His decrees, His creation, His laws, His providences—cannot be otherwise than good: as it is written, "And God saw everything that He had made, and, behold, it was very good" (Gen 1:31). Thus, the goodness of God is seen, first, in creation. The more closely the creature is studied, the more the beneficence of its Creator becomes apparent. Take the highest of God's earthly creatures—man. Abundant reason has he to say with the Psalmist, "I will praise You, for I am fearfully and wonderfully made: marvelous are Your works; and that my soul knows right well" (139:14). Everything about the structure of our bodies attest to the goodness of their Maker. How suited the hands to perform their allotted work! How good of the Lord to appoint sleep to refresh the wearied body! How benevolent His provision to give to the eyes lids and brows for their protection! And so we might continue indefinitely.

Nor is the goodness of the Creator confined to man; it is exercised toward all His creatures. "The eyes of all wait upon You; and You give them their food in due season. You open Your hand, and satisfy the desire of every living thing" (Psalm 145:15,16). Whole volumes might be written, yes have been, to amplify this fact. Whether it be the birds of the air, the beasts of the forest, or the fish in the sea—abundant provision has been made to supply their every need. God "gives food to all flesh, for His mercy endures forever" (Psalm 136:25). Truly, "The earth is full of the goodness of the Lord" (Psalm 33:5).

The goodness of God is seen in the variety of natural pleasures which He has provided for His creatures. God might have been pleased to satisfy our hunger without the food being pleasing to our palates—how His benevolence appears in the varied flavors which He has given to meats, vegetables, and fruits! God has not only given us senses, but also that which gratifies them; and this too reveals His goodness. The earth might have been as fertile as it is without its surface being so delightfully variegated. Our physical lives could have been sustained without beautiful flowers to regale our eyes with their colors, and our nostrils with their sweet perfumes. We might have walked the fields without our ears being saluted by the music the birds. Whence, then, this loveliness, this charm, so freely diffused over the face of nature? Truly, "The Lord is good to everyone. He showers compassion on all his creation" (Psalm 145:9).

The goodness of God is seen in that when man transgressed the law of His Creator a dispensation of unmixed wrath did not at once commence. Well might God have deprived His fallen creatures of every blessing, every comfort, every pleasure. Instead, He ushered in a regime of a mixed nature— of mercy and judgment. This is very wonderful if it be duly considered, and the more thoroughly that regime be expanded the more will it appear that "mercy rejoices over judgment" (James 2:13). Notwithstanding all the evils which attend our fallen state, the balance of good greatly preponderates. With comparatively rare exceptions, men and women experience a far greater number of days of health than they do of sickness and pain. There is much more creature-happiness than creature-misery in the world. Even our sorrows admit of considerable alleviation, and God has given to the human mind a pliability which adapts itself to circumstances and makes the most of them.

Nor can the benevolence of God be justly called into question because there is suffering and sorrow in the world. If man sins against the goodness of God, if he despises "the riches of His goodness and forbearance and longsuffering, and after the hardness and impenitency of his heart treasures up unto himself wrath against the day of wrath" (Rom 2:4,5), who is to blame but himself? Would God be "good" if He did not punish those who ill-use His blessings, abuse His benevolence, and trample His mercies beneath their feet? It will be no reflection upon God's goodness, but rather the brightest exemplification of it, when He shall rid the earth of those who have broken His laws, defied His authority, mocked His messengers, scorned His Son, and persecuted those for whom He died.

The goodness of God appeared most illustriously when He sent forth His Son "made of a woman, made under the law, to redeem those who were under the law, that we might receive the adoption of sons" (Gal 4:4,5). Then it was that a multitude of the heavenly angels praised their Maker and said, "Glory to God in the highest heaven, and peace on earth to all whom God favors" (Luke 2:14). Yes, in the Gospel the "grace [which word in Greek conveys the idea if benevolence or goodness] of God that brings salvation has appeared to all men" (Titus 2:11). Nor can God's benignity be called into question because He has not made every sinful creature to be a subject of His redemptive grace. He did not bestow it upon the fallen angels. Had God left all to perish it would have been no reflection on His goodness. To any who would challenge this statement we will remind him of our Lord's sovereign prerogative: "Is it not lawful for Me to do what I will with My own? Is your eye evil, because I am good?" (Matt 20,15).

"Oh that men would praise the Lord for His goodness, and for His wonderful works to the children of men!" (Psalm 107:8). Gratitude is the return justly required from the objects of His beneficence, yet is it often withheld from our great Benefactor simply because His goodness is so constant and so abundant. It is lightly esteemed because it is exercised toward us in the common course of events. It is not felt because we daily experience it. "Do you despise the riches of His goodness?" (Rom 2:4). His goodness is "despised" when it is not improved as a means to lead men to repentance, but, on the contrary, serves to harden them from the supposition that God entirely overlooks their sin.

The goodness of God is the life of the believer's trust. It is this excellency in God which most appeals to our hearts. Because His goodness endures forever, we ought never to be discouraged: "The Lord is good, a stronghold in the day of trouble, and He knows those who trust in Him" (Nahum 1:7).

"When others behave badly to us, it should only stir us up the more heartily to give thanks unto the Lord, because He is good; and when we ourselves are conscious that we are far from being good, we should only the more reverently bless Him that He is good. We must never tolerate an instant's unbelief as to the goodness of the Lord; whatever else may be questioned, this is absolutely certain, that Jehovah is good; His dispensations may vary—but His nature is always the same" (C. H. Spurgeon).

CHAPTER 12
The Patience of God

Far less has been written upon this than the other excellencies of the divine character. Not a few of those who have expatiated at length upon the divine attributes have passed over the patience of God without any comment. It is not easy to suggest a reason for this, for surely the patience of God is as much one of the divine perfections as is His wisdom, power, or holiness, and as much to be admired and revered by us. True, the actual term will not be found in a concordance as frequently as the others, but the glory of this grace itself shines forth on almost every page of Scripture. Certain it is that we lose much if we do not frequently meditate upon the patience of God and earnestly pray that our hearts and ways may be more completely conformed thereto.

Most probably the principal reason why so many writers have failed to give us anything, separately, upon the patience of God was because of the difficulty of distinguishing this attribute from the divine goodness and mercy, particularly the latter. God's patience is mentioned in conjunction with His grace and mercy again and again, as may be seen by consulting Exodus 34:6, Numbers 14:18, Psalm 86:15, etc. That the patience of God is really a display of His mercy, that it is indeed one way in which it is frequently manifested, cannot be denied. But that patience and mercy are one and the same excellency, and are not to be separated, we cannot concede. It may not be easy to discriminate between them, nevertheless, Scripture fully warrants us in affirming some things about the one which we cannot about the other.

Stephen Charnock, the Puritan, defines God's patience, in part, thus: "It is part of the divine goodness and mercy, yet differs from both. God being the greatest goodness, has the greatest mildness; mildness is always the companion of true goodness, and the greater the goodness, the greater the mildness. Who so holy as Christ, and who so meek? God's slowness to anger is a branch ... from his mercy: 'The Lord is full of compassion, slow to anger' (Psalm 145:8). It differs from mercy in the formal consideration of the object

—mercy respects the creature as miserable, patience respects the creature as criminal; mercy pities him in his misery, and patience bears with the sin which engendered the misery, and is giving birth to more."

Personally, we would define the divine patience as that power of control which God exercises over Himself, causing Him to bear with the wicked and forbear so long in punishing them. In Nahum 1:3 we read, "The Lord is slow to anger and great in power," upon which Mr. Charnock said: "Men that are great in the world are quick in passion, and are not so ready to forgive an injury, or bear with an offender, as one of a lower rank. It is a lack of power over that man's self that makes him do unbecoming things upon a provocation. A prince that can bridle his passions is a king over himself as well as over his subjects. God is slow to anger because great in power. He has no less power over Himself than over His creatures."

It is at the above point, we think, that God's patience is most clearly distinguished from His mercy. Though the creature is benefited thereby, the patience of God chiefly respects Himself, a restraint placed upon His acts by His will; whereas His mercy terminates wholly upon the creature. The patience of God is that excellency which causes Him to sustain great injuries without immediately avenging Himself. He has a power of patience as well as a power of justice. Thus the Hebrew word for the divine patience or longsuffering is rendered "slow to anger" in Nehemiah 9:17, Psalm 103:8, etc. Not that there are any passions in the divine nature, but that God's wisdom and will is pleased to act with that stateliness and sobriety which is becoming to His exalted majesty.

In support of our definition above let us point out that it was to this excellency in the divine character that Moses appealed, when Israel sinned so grievously at Kadesh-Barnea, and there provoked Jehovah so sorely. Unto His servant the Lord said, "I will smite them with the pestilence and disinherit them." Then it was that the mediator Moses, as a type of the Christ to come, pleaded, "I beseech You, let the power of my Lord be great, according as You have spoken saying the Lord is patient" (Num 14:17). Thus, His "patience" is His "power' of self-restraint.

Again, in Romans 9:22 we read, "What if God, willing to show His wrath, and to make His power known, endured with much patience the vessels of wrath fitted to destruction." Were God to immediately break these reprobate vessels into pieces, His power of self-control would not so eminently appear; by bearing with their wickedness and forbearing punishment so long, the power of His patience is gloriously demonstrated. True, the wicked interpret His patience quite differently "because sentence against an evil work is not executed speedily, therefore the heart of the sons of men is fully set in them to do evil" (Eccl 8:11)—but the anointed eye adores what they abuse.

"The God of patience" (Rom 15:5) is one of the divine titles. Deity is thus denominated, first, because God is both the Author and Object of the grace of patience in the saint. Secondly, because this is what He is in Himself: patience is one of His perfections. Thirdly, as a pattern for us: "Therefore, as God's chosen people, holy and dearly loved, clothe yourselves with compassion, kindness, humility, gentleness and patience" (Col 3:12). And again, 'Be therefore followers [emulators] of God, as dear children" (Eph 5:1). When tempted to be disgusted at the dullness of another, or to be revenged on one who has wronged you, call to remembrance God's infinite patience and longsuffering with yourself.

The patience of God is manifested in His dealings with sinners. How strikingly was it displayed toward the antediluvians. When mankind was universally degenerate, and all flesh had corrupted its way, God did not destroy them until He had forewarned them. He "waited" (1 Peter 3:20), probably no less than 120 years (Gen 6:3), during which time Noah was a "preacher of righteousness" (2 Peter 2:5). So, later, when the Gentiles not only worshiped and served the creature more than the Creator, but also committed the vilest abominations contrary even to the dictates of nature (Rom 1:19-26) and thereby filled up the measure of their iniquity, yet, instead of drawing His sword for the extermination of such rebels, God "allowed all nations to walk in their own ways," and gave them "rain from heaven and fruitful seasons" (Acts 14:16,17).

Marvelously was God's patience exercised and manifested toward Israel. First, He "endured their conduct" for forty years in the wilderness (Acts 13:18). Later, when they had entered Canaan, but followed the evil customs of the nations around them, and turned to idolatry, though God chastened them sorely, He did not utterly destroy them, but in their distress, raised up deliverers for them. When their iniquity was raised to such a height that none but a God of infinite patience could have borne them, He spared them many years before He allowed them to be carried down into Babylon. Finally, when their rebellion against Him reached its climax by crucifying His Son, He waited forty years before He sent the Romans against them, and that, only after they had judged themselves "unworthy of everlasting life" (Acts

13:46).

How wondrous is God's patience with the world today. On every side people are sinning with a high hand. The divine law is trampled under foot and God Himself openly despised. It is truly amazing that He does not instantly strike dead those who so brazenly defy Him. Why does He not suddenly cut off the haughty infidel and blatant blasphemer, as He did Ananias and Sapphira? Why does He not cause the earth to open its mouth and devour the persecutors of His people, so that, like Dathan and Abiram, they shall go down alive into the bottomless pit? And what of apostate Christendom, where every possible form of sin is now tolerated and practiced under cover of the holy name of Christ? Why does not the righteous wrath of Heaven make an end of such abominations? Only one answer is possible: because God bears with "much patience the vessels of wrath fitted to destruction."

And what of the writer and the reader? Let us review our own lives. It is not long since we followed a multitude to do evil, had no concern for God's glory, and lived only to gratify self. How patiently He bore with our vile conduct! And now that grace has snatched us as brands from the burning, giving us a place in God's family, and has begotten us unto an eternal inheritance in glory, how miserably we requite Him. How shallow our gratitude, how tardy our obedience, how frequent our backslidings! One reason why God allows the flesh to remain in the believer is that He may exhibit His "patience to us" (2 Peter 3:9). Since this divine attribute is manifested only in this world, God takes advantage to display it toward "His own."

May our meditation upon this divine excellency soften our hearts, make our consciences tender, and may we learn in the school of holy experience the "patience of saints," namely, submission to the divine will and continuance in well doing. Let us earnestly seek grace to emulate this divine excellency. "Be therefore perfect, even as your Father who is in heaven is perfect" (Matt 5:48). In the immediate context of this verse Christ exhorts us to love our enemies, bless those who curse us, do good to those who hate us. God bears long with the wicked notwithstanding the multitude of their sins— and shall we desire to be revenged because of a single injury?

CHAPTER 13
The Grace of God

Grace is a perfection of the divine character which is exercised only toward the elect. Neither in the Old Testament nor in the New, is the grace of God ever mentioned in connection with mankind generally, still less with the lower orders of His creatures. In this it is distinguished from "mercy," for the mercy of God is "over all His works" (Psalm 145:9). Grace is the sole source from which flows the goodwill, love, and salvation of God unto His chosen people. This attribute of the divine character was defined by Abraham Booth in his helpful book "The Reign of Grace" thus: "It is the eternal and absolute free favor of God, manifested in the bestowment of spiritual and eternal blessings to the guilty and the unworthy."

Divine grace is the sovereign and saving favor of God exercised in the bestowment of blessings upon those who have no merit in them and for which no compensation is demanded from them. Nay, more; it is the favor of God shown to those who not only have no positive deserts of their own, but who are thoroughly ill-deserving and hell-deserving. It is completely unmerited and unsought, and is altogether unattracted by anything in or from or by the objects upon which it is bestowed. Grace can neither be bought, earned, nor won by the creature. If it could be, it would cease to be grace. When a thing is said to be of "grace," we mean that the recipient has no claim upon it, that it was in nowise due him. It comes to him as pure charity, and, at first, unasked and undesired.

The fullest exposition of the amazing grace of God is to be found in the Epistles of the Apostle Paul. In his writings "grace" stands in direct opposition to works and worthiness, all works and worthiness, of whatever kind or degree. This is abundantly clear from Romans 11:6, "And if by grace, then it is no longer by works; if it were, grace would no longer be grace." Grace and works will no more unite than an acid and an alkali. "By grace are you saved through faith; and that not of yourselves; it is the gift of God: not of works, lest any man should boast" (Eph 2:8,9). The absolute favor of God can no more consist with human merit than oil and water will fuse into one (see also Rom 4:4,5).

There are three principal CHARACTERISTICS of divine grace.

First, it is eternal. Grace was planned before it was exercised, purposed before it was imparted: "Who has saved us, and called us with a holy calling, not according to our works, but according to His own purpose and grace, which was given us in Christ Jesus before the world began" (2 Tim 1:9).

Secondly, it is free, for none did ever purchase it: "Being justified freely by His grace" (Rom 3:24).

Thirdly, it is sovereign, because God exercises it toward and bestows it upon whom He pleases: "Even so might grace reign" (Rom 5:21). If grace "reigns" then it is on the throne, and the occupant of the throne is sovereign. Hence "the throne of grace" (Heb 4:16).

Just because grace is unmerited favor, it must be exercised in a sovereign manner. Therefore does the Lord declare, "I will be gracious to whom I will be gracious" (Exo 33:19). Were God to show grace to all of Adam's descendants, men would at once conclude that He was righteously compelled to take them to heaven as a fit compensation for allowing the human race to fall into sin. But the great God is under no obligation to any of His creatures, least of all to those who are rebels against Him.

Eternal life is a gift, therefore it can neither be earned by good works, nor claimed as a right. Seeing that salvation is a "gift," who has any right to tell God on whom He ought to bestow it? It is not that the Giver ever refuses this gift to any who seek it wholeheartedly, and according to the rules which He has prescribed. No! He refuses none who come to Him empty-handed, and in the way of His appointing. But if out of a world of impenitent and unbelieving rebels, God is determined to exercise His sovereign right by choosing a limited number to be saved, who is wronged? Is God obliged to force His gift on those who value it not? Is God compelled to save those who are determined to go their own way?

But nothing more riles the natural man, and brings to the surface his innate and inveterate enmity against God, than to press upon him the eternality, the freeness, and the absolute sovereignty of divine grace. That God should have formed His purpose from everlasting, without in any way consulting the creature, is too abasing for the unbroken heart. That grace cannot be earned or won by any efforts of man is too self-emptying for self-righteousness. And that grace singles out whom it pleases to be its favored object arouses hot protests from haughty rebels. The clay rises up against the Potter and asks, "Why have You made me thus?" A lawless insurrectionist dares to call into question the justice of divine sovereignty.

The distinguishing grace of God is seen in saving those people whom He has sovereignly singled out to be His high favorites. By "distinguishing" we mean that grace discriminates, makes differences, chooses some and passes by others. It was distinguishing grace which selected Abraham from the midst of his idolatrous neighbors and made him "the friend of God." It was distinguishing grace which saved "publicans and sinners," but said of the religious Pharisees, "Let them alone" (Matt 15:14). Nowhere does the glory of God's free and sovereign grace shine more conspicuously than in the unworthiness and unlikeliness of its objects.

Beautifully was this illustrated by James Hervey, (1751): "Where sin has abounded, says the proclamation from the court of heaven, grace does much more abound. Manasseh was a monster of barbarity, for he caused his own children to pass through the fire, and filled Jerusalem with innocent blood. Manasseh was an adept in iniquity, for he not only multiplied, and to an extravagant degree, his own sacrilegious impieties, but he poisoned the principles and perverted the manners of his subjects, making them do worse than the most detestable of the heathen idolaters (see 2 Chron 33). Yet, through this superabundant grace he is humbled, he is reformed, and becomes a child of forgiving love, an heir of immortal glory."

Behold that bitter and bloody persecutor, Saul, when, breathing out threatenings and bent upon slaughter, he worried the lambs and put to death the disciples of Jesus. The havoc he had committed, the innocent families he had already ruined, were not sufficient to assuage his vengeful spirit. They were only a taste, which, instead of glutting the bloodhound, made him more closely pursue the track, and more eagerly pant for destruction. He is still athirst for violence and murder. So eager and insatiable is his thirst, that he even breathes out threatening and slaughter (Acts 9:1). His words are spears and arrows, and his tongue a sharp sword. It is as natural for him to harm the Christians, as to breathe the air. Nay, they bled every hour in the purposes of his rancorous heart. It is only owing to lack of power that every syllable he utters, every breath he draws, does not deal out deaths, and cause some of the innocent disciples to fall. Who, upon the principles of human judgment, would not have pronounced him a vessel of wrath, destined to unavoidable damnation? Nay, who would not have been ready to conclude that, if there were heavier chains and a deeper dungeon in the world of woe, they must surely be reserved for such an implacable enemy of true godliness? Yet, admire and adore the inexhaustible treasures of grace—this Saul is admitted into the holy fellowship of the prophets, is numbered with the noble army of martyrs and makes a distinguished figure among the glorious company of the apostles.

The Corinthians were flagitious even to a proverb. Some of them wallowed in such abominable vices, and habituated themselves to such outrageous acts of injustice, as were a reproach to human nature. Yet even these sons of violence and slaves of sensuality were washed, sanctified, justified (1 Cor 6:9-11). "Washed," in the precious blood of a dying Redeemer; "sanctified," by the powerful operations of the blessed Spirit, "justified," through the infinitely tender mercies of a gracious God. Those who were once the burden of the earth—are now the joy of heaven, the delight of angels.

Now the grace of God is manifested in and by and through the Lord Jesus Christ. "The law was given by Moses, but grace and truth came by Jesus Christ" (John 1:17). This does not mean that God never exercised grace toward any before His Son became incarnate; Genesis 6:8, Exodus 33:19, etc., clearly show otherwise. But grace and truth were fully revealed and perfectly exemplified when the Redeemer came to this earth, and died for His people upon the cross. It is through Christ the Mediator alone that the grace of God flows to His elect. "Much more the grace of God, and the gift of grace, which is by one man, Jesus Christ ... much more those who receive abundance of grace, and of the gift of righteousness, shall reign in life by one, Jesus Christ ... so might grace reign through righteousness unto eternal life by Jesus Christ our Lord" (Rom 5:15,17,21).

The grace of God is proclaimed in the Gospel (Acts 20:24), which is to the self-righteous Jew a "stumbling block," and to the conceited and philosophizing Greek "foolishness." And why so? Because there is nothing whatever in it that is adapted to the gratifying of the pride of man. It announces that unless we are saved by grace, we cannot be saved at all. It declares that apart from Christ, the unspeakable Gift of God's grace, the state of every man is desperate, irremediable, hopeless. The Gospel addresses men as guilty, condemned, perishing criminals. It declares that the most chaste moralist is in the same terrible plight as is the most voluptuous profligate; and the zealous professor, with all his religious performances, is no better off than the most profane infidel.

The Gospel contemplates every descendant of Adam as a fallen, polluted, hell-deserving and helpless sinner. The grace which the Gospel publishes is his only hope. All stand before God convicted as transgressors of His holy law, as guilty and condemned criminals, who are not merely awaiting sentence, but the execution of the sentence already passed upon them (John 3:18; Rom 3:19). To complain against the partiality of grace is suicidal. If the sinner insists upon bare justice, then the Lake of Fire must be his eternal portion. His only hope lies in bowing to the sentence which divine justice has passed upon him, owning the absolute righteousness of it, casting himself on the mercy of God, and stretching forth empty hands to avail himself of the grace of God now made known to him in the Gospel.

The Holy Spirit is the Communicator of grace, therefore is He denominated "the Spirit of grace" (Zech 12:10). God the Father is the Fountain of all grace, for He purposed in Himself the everlasting covenant of redemption. God the Son is the only Channel of grace. The Gospel is the Publisher of grace. The Spirit is the Bestower. He is the One who applies the Gospel in saving power to the soul: quickening the elect while spiritually dead, conquering their rebellious wills, melting their hard hearts, opening their blind eyes, cleansing them from the leprosy of sin. Thus we may say with the late G. S. Bishop: "Grace is a provision for men who are so fallen that they cannot lift the axe of justice, so corrupt that they cannot change their own natures, so averse to God that they cannot turn to Him, so blind that they cannot see Him, so deaf that they cannot hear Him, and so dead that He Himself must open their graves and lift them into resurrection."

CHAPTER 14
The Mercy of God

"O give thanks unto the Lord: for He is good: for His mercy endures forever" (Psalm 136:1). For this perfection of the divine character, God is greatly to be praised. Three times over in as many verses does the Psalmist here call upon the saints to give thanks unto the Lord for this adorable attribute. And surely this is the least that can be asked for from those who have been recipients of such bounty. When we contemplate the characteristics of this divine excellency, we cannot do otherwise than bless God for it. His mercy is "great" (1 Kings 3:6), "plenteous" (Psalm 86:5), "tender" (Luke 1:78), "abundant" (1 Peter 1:3); it is "from everlasting to everlasting upon those who fear Him" (Psalm 103:17). Well may we say with the Psalmist, "I will sing aloud of Your mercy" (59:16).

"I will make all My goodness pass before you, and I will proclaim the name of the Lord before you; and will be gracious to whom I will be gracious, and will show mercy on whom I will show mercy" (Exo 33:19). Wherein differs the "mercy" of God from His "grace"? The mercy of God has its spring in the divine goodness. The first issue of God's goodness is His benignity or bounty, by which He gives liberally to His creatures as creatures; thus has He given being and life to all things. The second issue of God's goodness is His mercy, which denotes the ready inclination of God to relieve the misery of fallen creatures. Thus, mercy presupposes sin.

Though it may not be easy at the first consideration to perceive a real difference between the grace and the mercy of God, it helps us thereto if we carefully ponder His dealings with the unfallen angels. He has never exercised mercy toward them, for they have never stood in any need thereof, not having sinned or come beneath the effects of the curse. Yet, they certainly are the objects of God's free and sovereign grace.

First, because of His election of them from out of the whole angelic race (1 Tim 5:21).

Secondly, and in consequence of their election, because of His preservation of them from apostasy, when Satan rebelled and dragged down with him one-third of the celestial multitude (Rev 12:4).

Thirdly, in making Christ their Head (Col 2:10; 1 Peter 3:22), whereby they are eternally secured in the holy condition in which they were created.

Fourthly, because of the exalted position which has been assigned them: to live in God's immediate presence (Dan 7:10), to serve Him constantly in His heavenly temple, to receive honorable commissions from Him (Heb 1:14). This is abundant grace toward them; but "mercy" it is not.

In endeavoring to study the mercy of God as it is set forth in Scripture, a threefold distinction needs to be made, if the Word of Truth is to be "rightly divided" thereon.

First, there is a general mercy of God, which is extended not only to all men, believers and unbelievers alike, but also to the entire creation: "His tender mercies are over all His works" (Psalm 145:9); "He gives to all life, and breath, and all things" (Acts 17:25). God has pity upon the brute creation in their need, and supplies them with suitable provision.

Secondly, there is a special mercy of God, which is exercised toward the children of men, helping and supporting them, notwithstanding their sins. To them also He communicates all the necessities of life: "for He makes His sun to rise on the evil and on the good, and sends rain on the just and on the unjust" (Matt 5.45).

Thirdly, there is a sovereign mercy which is reserved for the heirs of salvation, which is communicated to them in a covenant way, through the Mediator.

Following out a little further the difference between the second and third distinctions pointed out above, it is important to note that the mercies which God bestows on the wicked are solely of a temporal nature; that is to say, they are confined strictly to this present life. There will be no mercy extended to them beyond the grave: "It is a people of no understanding: therefore He who made them will not have mercy on them, and He who formed them will show them no favor" (Isa 27.11). But at this point a difficulty may suggest itself to some of our readers, namely, Does not Scripture affirm that "His mercy endures forever" (Psalm 136:1)? Two things need to be pointed out in that connection. God can never cease to be merciful, for this is a quality of the divine essence (Psalm 116:5); but the exercise of His mercy is regulated by His sovereign will. This must be so, for there is nothing outside Himself which obliges Him to act; if there were, that "something" would be supreme, and God would cease to be God.

It is pure sovereign grace which alone determines the exercise of divine mercy. God expressly affirms this fact in Romans 9:15, "I will have mercy on whom I will have mercy." It is not the wretchedness of the creature which causes Him to show mercy, for God is not influenced by things outside of Himself as we are. If God were influenced by the abject misery of leprous sinners, He would cleanse and save all of them. But He does not. Why? Simply because it is not His pleasure and purpose so to do. Still less is it the merits of the creatures which causes Him to bestow mercies upon them, for it is a contradiction in terms to speak of meriting "mercy." "Not by works of righteousness which we have done, but according to His mercy He saved us" (Titus 3:5)—the one standing in direct antithesis to the other. Nor is it the merit of Christ which moves God to bestow mercies on His elect: that would be substituting the effect for the cause. It is "through" or because of the tender mercy of our God that Christ was sent here to His people (Luke 1:78). The merits of Christ make it possible for God to righteously bestow spiritual mercies on His elect, justice having been fully satisfied by the Surety! Divine mercy arises solely from God's imperial pleasure.

Again, though it be true, blessedly and gloriously true, that God's mercy "endures forever," yet we must observe carefully the objects to whom His "mercy" is shown. Even the casting of the reprobate into the Lake of Fire is an act of mercy. The punishment of the wicked is to be contemplated from a threefold viewpoint. From God's side, it is an act of justice, vindicating His honor. The mercy of God is never shown to the prejudice of His holiness and righteousness. From their side, it is an act of equity, when they are made to suffer the due reward of their iniquities. But from the standpoint of the redeemed, the punishment of the wicked is an act of unspeakable mercy. How dreadful would it be if the present order of things, when the children of God are obliged to live in the midst of the children of the Devil, should continue forever! Heaven would at once cease to be heaven if the ears of the saints still heard the blasphemous and filthy language of the reprobate. What a mercy that in Heaven, "Nothing evil will be allowed to enter—no one who practices shameful idolatry and dishonesty—but only those whose names are written in the Lamb's Book of Life!" (Rev 21:27)

Lest the reader might think in the last paragraph we have been drawing upon our imagination, let us appeal to Holy Scripture in support of what has been said. In Psalm 143:12 we find David praying, "And of Your mercy cut off my enemies, and destroy all those who afflict my soul: for I am Your servant." Again, in Psalm 136:15 we read that God "overthrew Pharaoh and his army in the Red Sea—for His mercy endures forever." It was an act of vengeance upon Pharaoh and his army, but it was an act of mercy unto the Israelites.

Again, in Revelation 19:1-3 we read: "After this I heard what sounded like the roar of a great multitude in heaven shouting: Hallelujah! Salvation and glory and power belong to our God, for true and just are his judgments. He has condemned the great prostitute who corrupted the earth by her adulteries. He has avenged on her the blood of his servants. And again they shouted—Hallelujah! The smoke from her goes up for ever and ever."

From what has just been before us, let us note how vain is the presumptuous hope of the wicked, who, notwithstanding their continued defiance of God, nevertheless count upon His being merciful to them. How many there are who say, I do not believe that God will ever cast me into Hell; He is too merciful. Such a hope is a viper, which if cherished in their bosoms will sting them to death. God is a God of justice as well as mercy, and He has expressly declared that He will "by no means clear the guilty" (Exo 34:7). Yes, He has said, "The wicked shall be turned into hell, and all the nations that forget God" (Psalm 9:17). As well might men reason thus: I do not believe that if filth is allowed to accumulate and sewage become stagnant and people deprive themselves of fresh air, that a merciful God will let them fall a prey to a deadly fever. The fact is that those who neglect the laws of health are carried away by disease, notwithstanding God's mercy. Equally true is it that those who neglect the laws of spiritual health, shall forever suffer the second death.

Unspeakably solemn is it to see so many abusing this divine perfection. They continue to despise God's authority, trample upon His laws, continue in sin—and yet presume upon His mercy! But God will not be unjust to Himself. God shows mercy to the truly penitent, but not to the impenitent (Luke 13:3). To continue in sin and yet reckon upon divine mercy remitting punishment is diabolical. It is saying, "Let us do evil that good may come," and of all such it is written that their "damnation is just" (Rom 3:8). Presumption shall most certainly be disappointed; read carefully Deuteronomy 29:18-20. Christ is the spiritual Mercy seat, and all who despise and reject His Lordship shall "be destroyed in your way, for his wrath can flare up in a moment" (Psalm 2:12).

But let our final thought be of God's spiritual mercies unto His own people. "Your mercy is great unto the heavens" (Psalm 57:10). The riches thereof transcend our loftiest thought. "For as the heaven is high above the earth, so great is His mercy toward those who fear Him" (Psalm 103:11). None can measure it. The elect are designated "vessels of mercy" (Rom 9:23). It is mercy which quickened them when they were dead in sins (Eph 2:4,5). It is mercy which saves them (Titus 3:5). It is His abundant mercy which begat them unto an eternal inheritance (1 Peter 1:3). Time would fail us to tell of His preserving, sustaining, pardoning, supplying mercy. Unto His own, God is "the Father of mercies" (2 Cor 1:3).

"When all Your mercies, O my God,
My rising soul surveys,
Transported with the view I'm lost,
In wonder, love, and praise."

CHAPTER 15
The Loving-kindness of God

We propose to engage the reader with another of His excellencies—of which every Christian receives innumerable proofs. We turn to a consideration of God's loving-kindness because our aim is to maintain a due proportion in treating of the divine perfections, for all of us are apt to entertain one-sided views of them. A balance must be preserved here (as everywhere), as it appears in those two statements of the divine attributes, "God is light" (1 John 1:5), "God is love" (1 John 4:8). The sterner, more awe-inspiring aspects of the divine character are offset by the gentler, more winsome ones. It is to our irreparable loss if we dwell exclusively on God's sovereignty and majesty, or His holiness and justice; we need to meditate frequently, though not exclusively, on His goodness and mercy. Nothing short of a full-orbed view of the divine perfection revealed in Holy Writ, should satisfy us.

Scripture speaks of "the multitude of His lovingkindnesses," and who is capable of numbering them? (Isa 63:7). Said the Psalmist, "How excellent is Your loving-kindness, O God!" (36:7). No pen of man, no tongue of angel, can adequately express it. Familiar as this blessed attribute of God's may be to people, it is something entirely peculiar to divine revelation. None of the ancients ever dreamed of investing his "gods" with such endearing perfection as this. None of the objects worshiped by present-day heathen possess gentleness and tenderness; very much the reverse is true, as the hideous features of their idols exhibit. Philosophers regard it as a serious reflection upon the honor of the Absolute to ascribe such qualities to it. But the Scriptures have much to say about God's loving-kindness, or His paternal favor to His people, His tender affection toward them.

The first time this divine perfection is mentioned in the Word is in that wondrous manifestation of Deity to Moses, when Jehovah proclaimed His "Name," that is, Himself as made known. "The Lord, the Lord God, merciful and gracious, longsuffering, and abundant in goodness and truth" (Exo 34:6), though much more frequently the Hebrew word, chesed, is rendered "kindness" and "loving-kindness." In our English Bibles the initial reference, as connected with God, is Psalm 17:7, where David prayed, "Show Your marvelous loving-kindness, O You who save by your right hand those who take refuge in you from their foes." Marvelous it is, that One so infinitely above us, so inconceivably glorious, so ineffably holy, should not only notice such worms of the earth, but also set His heart upon them, give His Son for them, send His Spirit to indwell them, and so bear with all their imperfections and waywardness as never to remove His loving-kindness from them.

Consider some of the evidences and exercises of this divine attribute unto the saints, "In love having predestinated us unto the adoption of children by Jesus Christ to Himself" (Eph 1:4,5). As the previous verse shows, that love was engaged in their behalf before this world came into existence. "This is how God showed His love among us: He sent His one and only Son into the world that we might live through Him" (1 John 4:9), which was His amazing provision for us fallen creatures. "I have loved you with an everlasting love: therefore with loving-kindness have I drawn you" (Jer 31:3), by the quickening operations of My Spirit, by the invincible power of My grace, by creating in you a deep sense of need, by attracting you by My winsomeness. "I will take you to be My wife forever. I will take you to be My wife in righteousness, justice, love, and compassion." (Hosea 2:19). Having made us willing in the day of His power to give ourselves to Him, the Lord enters into an everlasting marriage contract with us!

This loving-kindness of the Lord is never removed from His children. To our reason it may appear to be so, yet it never is. Since the believer is in Christ, nothing can separate him from the love of God (Rom 8:39). God has solemnly engaged Himself by covenant, and our sins cannot make it void. God has sworn that if His children keep not His commandments He will "visit their transgression with the rod, and their iniquity with stripes." Yet He adds, "Nevertheless My loving-kindness will I not utterly take from him, nor allow my faithfulness to fail. My covenant will I not break" (Psalm 89:31-34). Observe the change of number from "their" and "them" to "Him." The loving-kindness of God toward His people is centered in Christ. Because His exercise of loving-kindness is a covenant engagement it is repeatedly linked to His "truth" (Psalm 40:11; 138:2), showing that it proceeds to us by promise. Therefore we should never despair.

"Though the mountains be shaken and the hills be removed, yet my unfailing love for you will not be shaken nor my covenant of peace be removed," says the Lord, who has compassion on you" (Isa 54:10). No, that covenant has been ratified by the blood of its Mediator, by which blood the enmity (occasioned by sin) has been removed, and perfect reconciliation effected. God knows the thoughts which He entertains for those embraced in His covenant and who have been reconciled to Him; namely, "thoughts of peace, and not of evil" (Jer 29:11). Therefore we are assured, "The Lord will command His loving-kindness in the daytime, and in the night His song shall be with me" (Psalm 42:8). What a word that is! Not merely that the Lord will give or bestow, but command His loving-kindness. It is given by decree, bestowed by royal engagement, as He also commands "deliverances ... the blessing, even life for evermore" (Psalm 44:4; 133:3), which announces that nothing can possibly hinder these bestowments. What ought our response to be?

First, "Be therefore imitators of God as dear children; and walk in love" (Eph 5:1,2). "Therefore, as God's chosen people, holy and dearly loved, clothe yourselves with compassion, kindness, humility, gentleness and patience" (Col 3:12). Thus it was with David: "Your loving-kindness is before my eyes: and I have walked in Your truth" (Psalm 26:3). He delighted to ponder it. It refreshed his soul to do so, and it molded his conduct. The more we are occupied with God's goodness, the more careful we will be about our obedience. The constraints of God's love and grace are more powerful to the regenerate than the terrors of His Law. "How excellent is Your loving-kindness, O God! therefore the children of men put their trust under the shadow of Your wings" (Psalm 36:7).

Second, a sense of this divine perfection strengthens our faith, and promotes confidence in God.

Third, it should stimulate the spirit of worship. "Because Your loving-kindness is better than life, my lips shall praise You (Psalm 63:3; cf 138:2).

Fourth, it should be our cordial when downcast. "Let ... Your merciful kindness be for my comfort" (Psalm 119:76). It was so with Christ in His anguish (Psalm 69:17).

Fifth, it should be our plea in prayer, "Quicken me, O Lord, according to Your loving-kindness" (Psalm 119:159). David applied to that divine attribute for new strength and increased vigor.

Sixth, we should appeal to it when we have fallen by the wayside. "Have mercy upon me, O God, according to Your loving-kindness" (Psalm 51:1).

Deal with him according to the gentlest of Your attributes, make my case an exemplification of Your tenderness.

Seventh, it should be a petition in our evening devotions. "Cause me to hear Your loving-kindness in the morning" (Psalm 143:8). Arouse me with my soul in tune therewith, let my waking thoughts be of Your goodness.

CHAPTER 16
The Love of God

There are three things told us in Scripture concerning the nature of God.

First, "God is spirit" (John 4:24). In the Greek there is no indefinite article, and to say "God is a spirit" is most objectionable, for it places Him in a class with others. God is "spirit" in the highest sense. Because He is "spirit" He is incorporeal, having no visible substance. Had God a tangible body, He would not be omnipresent, He would be limited to one place; because He is "spirit" He fills heaven and earth.

Secondly, "God is light" (1 John 1:5), which is the opposite of darkness. In Scripture "darkness" stands for sin, evil, death, and "light" for holiness, goodness, life. "God is light" means that He is the sum of all excellency.

Thirdly, "God is love" (1 John 4:8). It is not simply that God "loves," but that He is Love itself. Love is not merely one of His attributes, but His very nature.

There are many today who talk about the love of God, who are total strangers to the God of love. The divine love is commonly regarded as a species of amiable weakness, a sort of good-natured indulgence; it is reduced to a mere sickly sentiment, patterned after human emotion. Now the truth is that on this, as on everything else, our thoughts need to be formed and regulated by what is revealed thereon in Holy Scripture. That there is urgent need for this is apparent not only from the ignorance which so generally prevails, but also the low state of spirituality which is now so sadly evident everywhere among professing Christians. How little real love there is for God. One chief reason for this is because our hearts are so little occupied with His wondrous love for His people. The better we are acquainted with His love—its character, fullness, blessedness the more will our hearts be drawn out in love to Him.

1. The love of God is UNINFLUENCED. By this we mean, there was nothing whatever in the objects of His love to call it into exercise, nothing in the creature to attract or prompt it. The love which one creature has for

another is because of something in the object; but the love of God is free, spontaneous, uncaused. The only reason why God loves any, is found in His own sovereign will: "The Lord did not set His love upon you, nor choose you, because you were more in number than any people; for you were the fewest of all people: but because the Lord loved you" (Deut 7:7-8). God has loved His people from everlasting, and therefore nothing about the creature can be the cause of what is found in God from eternity. He loves from Himself "according to His own purpose" (2 Tim 1:9).

"We love Him, because He first loved us" (1 John 4:19). God did not love us because we loved Him; but He loved us before we had a particle of love for Him. Had God loved us in return for ours, then it would not be spontaneous on His part; but because He loved us when we were loveless, it is clear that His love was uninfluenced. It is highly important, if God is to be honored and the heart of His child established, that we should be quite clear upon this precious truth. God's love for me and for each of "His own" was entirely unmoved by anything in us. What was there in me to attract the heart of God? Absolutely nothing. But, to the contrary, there was everything to repel Him, everything calculated to make Him loathe me—sinful, depraved, a mass of corruption, with "no good thing" in me.

"What was there in me that could merit esteem,
Or give the Creator delight?
'Twas even so, Father, I ever must sing,
Because it seemed good in Your sight."

2. The love of God is ETERNAL. This is of necessity. God Himself is eternal, and God is love; therefore, as God Himself had no beginning, His love had none. Granted that such a concept far transcends the grasp of our feeble minds, nevertheless, where we cannot comprehend we can bow in adoring worship. How clear is the testimony of Jeremiah 31:3, "I have loved you with an everlasting love: therefore with loving-kindness have I drawn you." How blessed to know that the great and holy God loved His people before heaven and earth were called into existence, that He had set His heart upon them from all eternity. Clear proof is this that His love is spontaneous, for He loved them endless ages before they had any being.

The same precious truth is set forth in Ephesians 1:4-5: "According as He has chosen us in Him before the foundation of the world, that we should be holy and without blame before Him. In love having predestinated us." What praise should this evoke from each of His children! How tranquilizing for the heart: since God's love toward me had no beginning, it can have no ending! Since it is true that "from everlasting to everlasting" He is God, and since God is "love," then it is equally true that "from everlasting to everlasting" He loves His people.

3. The love of God is SOVEREIGN. This also is self-evident. God Himself is sovereign, under obligations to none, a law unto Himself, acting always according to His own imperial pleasure. Since God is sovereign, and since He is love, it necessarily follows that His love is sovereign. Because God is God, He does as He pleases; because God is love, He loves whom He pleases. Such is His own express affirmation: "Jacob have I loved, but Esau have I hated" (Rom 9:13). There was no more reason in Jacob why he should be the object of divine love than there was in Esau. They both had the same parents, and were born at the same time, being twins; yet God loved the one and hated the other! Why? Because it pleased Him to do so.

The sovereignty of God's love necessarily follows from the fact that it is uninfluenced by anything in the creature. Thus, to affirm that the cause of His love lies in God Himself is only another way of saying, He loves whom He pleases. For a moment, assume the opposite. Suppose God's love were regulated by anything else than His will: in such a case He would love by rule, and loving by rule He would be under a law of love, and then so far from being free, God would Himself be ruled by Law. "In love having predestinated us unto the adoption of children by Jesus Christ to Himself, according to"—what? Some excellency which He foresaw in them? No! What then? "According to the good pleasure of His will" (Eph 1:4-5).

4. The love of God is INFINITE. Everything about God is infinite. His essence fills heaven and earth. His wisdom is illimitable, for He knows everything of the past, present, and future. His power is unbounded, for there is nothing too hard for Him. So His love is without limit. There is a depth to it which none can fathom; there is a height to it which none can scale; there is a length and breadth to it which defies measurement, by any creature standard. Beautifully is this intimated in Ephesians 2:4: "But God, who is rich in mercy, for His great love wherewith He loved us": the word "great" there is parallel with the word "so" in John 3:16—"God so loved." It tells us that the love of God is so transcendent it cannot be estimated.

"No tongue can fully express the infinitude of God's love, or any mind comprehend it: it 'passes knowledge' (Eph 3:19). The most extensive ideas that a finite mind can frame about divine love, are infinitely below its true nature. The heaven is not so far above the earth as the goodness of God is beyond the most raised conceptions which we are able to form of it. God's love is an ocean which swells higher than all the mountains of opposition in such as are the objects of it. It is a fountain from which flows all necessary good to all those who are interested in it" (John Brine, 1743).

5. The love of God is IMMUTABLE. As with God Himself there is "no variableness, neither shadow of turning" (James 1:17), so His love knows neither change nor diminution. The worm Jacob supplies a forceful example of this: "Jacob have I loved," declared Jehovah, and despite all his unbelief and waywardness, He never ceased to love him. John 13:1 furnishes another beautiful illustration. That very night one of the apostles would say, "Show us the Father"; another would deny Him with cursings; all of them would be scandalized by, and forsake Him. Nevertheless, "having loved His own which were in the world, He loved them unto the end." The divine love is subject to no vicissitudes. Divine love is "strong as death." "Many waters cannot quench love, neither can the floods drown it" (Song 8:6-7). Nothing can separate from it (Rom 8:35-39).

"His love no end nor measure knows,
No change can turn its course,
Eternally the same it flows
From one eternal source."

6. The love of God is HOLY. God's love is not regulated by caprice, passion, or sentiment, but by principle. Just as His grace reigns not at the expense of it, but "through righteousness" (Rom 5:21), so His love never conflicts with His holiness. "God is light" (1 John 1:5) is mentioned before "God is love" (1 John 4:8). God's love is no mere amiable weakness or effeminate softness. Scripture declares that "whom the Lord loves He chastens, and scourges every son whom He receives" (Heb 12:6). God will not wink at sin, even in His own people. His love is pure, unmixed with any mushy sentimentality.

7. The love of God is GRACIOUS. The love and favor of God are inseparable. This is clearly brought out in Romans 8:32-39. What that love is, from which there can be no "separation," is easily perceived from the design and scope of the immediate context: it is that goodwill and grace of God which determined Him to give His Son for sinners. That love was the impulsive power of Christ's incarnation: "God so loved the world that He gave His only begotten Son" (John 3:16). Christ died not in order to make

God love us, but because He did love His people. Calvary is the supreme demonstration of divine love. Whenever you are tempted to doubt the love of God, Christian reader—go back to Calvary.

Here then is abundant cause for trust and patience under divine affliction. Christ was beloved of the Father, yet He was not exempted from poverty, disgrace, and persecution. He hungered and thirsted. Thus, it was not incompatible with God's love for Christ when He permitted men to spit upon and smite Him. Then let no Christian call into question God's love when he is brought under painful afflictions and trials. God did not enrich Christ on earth with temporal prosperity, for He had nowhere to lay His head. But He did give Him the Spirit without measure (John 3:34). Learn then that spiritual blessings are the principal gifts of divine love. How blessed to know that when the world hates us, God loves us!

The Love of God to Us
By "us" we mean His people. Although we read of the love which is in Christ Jesus our Lord" (Rom 8:39), Holy Writ knows nothing of a love of God outside of Christ. "The Lord is good to all: and His tender mercies are over all His works" (Psalm 145:9), so that He provides the ravens with food. "He is kind unto the unthankful and to the evil" (Luke 6:35), and His providence ministers unto the just and the unjust (Matt 5:45). But His love is reserved for His elect. That is unequivocally established by its characteristics, for the attributes of His love are identical with Himself. Necessarily so, for "God is love." In making that postulate it is but another way to say God's love is like Himself, from everlasting to everlasting—immutable. Nothing is more absurd than to imagine that anyone beloved of God can eternally perish or shall ever experience His everlasting vengeance. Since the love of God is "in Christ Jesus," it was attracted by nothing in its objects, nor can it be repelled by anything in, of, or by them. "Having loved His own which were in the world, He loved them unto the end" (John 13:1). The "world" in John 3:16 is a general term used in contrast with the Jews, and the verse must be interpreted so as not to contradict Psalms 5:5; 6:7; John 3:36; Romans 9:13.

The chief design of God is to commend the love of God in Christ, for He is the sole channel through which it flows. The Son has not induced the Father to love His people, but rather was it His love for them which moved Him to give His Son for them. Ralph Erskine said: "God has taken a marvelous way to manifest His love. When He would show His power, He makes a world. When He would display His wisdom, He puts it in a frame and form that discovers its vastness. When He would manifest the grandeur and glory of His name, He makes a heaven, and puts angels and archangels, principalities and powers therein. And when He would manifest His love, what will He not do? God has taken a great and marvelous way of manifesting it in Christ: His person, His blood, His death, His righteousness."

"For no matter how many promises God has made, they are "Yes" in Christ." (2 Cor 1:20). As we were chosen in Christ (Eph 1:4), as we were accepted in Him (Eph 1:6), as our life is hidden in Him (Col 3:3), so are we beloved in Him—"the love of God which is in Christ Jesus": in Him as our Head and Husband, which is why nothing can separate us therefrom, for that union is indissoluble.

Nothing so warms the heart of the saint as a spiritual contemplation of God's love. As he is occupied with it, he is lifted outside of and above his wretched self. A believing apprehension fills the renewed soul with holy satisfaction, and makes him as happy as it is possible for one to be this side of heaven. To know and believe the love which God has toward me is both a pledge and a foretaste of heaven itself. Since God loves His people in Christ, it is not for any amiableness in or attraction about them: "Jacob have I loved." Yes, the naturally unattractive, yes, despicable, Jacob—"worm Jacob." Since God loves His people in Christ, it is not regulated by their fruitfulness, but is the same at all times. Because He loves them in Christ, the Father loves them as Christ. The time will come when His prayer will be answered, "that the world may know that You have sent Me, and have loved them, as You have loved Me" (John 17:23). Only faith can grasp those marvelous things, for neither reasoning nor feelings can do so. God loves us in Christ. What infinite delight the Father has as He beholds His people in His dear Son! All our blessings flow from that precious fountain.

God's love to His people is not of yesterday. It did not begin with their love to Him. No, "we love Him, because He first loved us" (1 John 4:19). We do not first give to Him, that He may return to us again. Our regeneration is not the motive of His love, rather His love is the reason why He renews us after His image. This is often made to appear in the first manifestation of it, when so far from its objects being engaged in seeking Him, they are at their worst.

"'Later I passed by, and when I looked at you and saw that you were old enough for love, I spread the corner of my garment over you and covered your nakedness. I gave you My solemn oath and entered into a covenant with you, declares the Sovereign Lord, and you became [manifestly] Mine" (Eze 16:8).

Not only are its objects often at their worst when God's love is first revealed to them, but actually doing their worst, as in the case of Saul of Tarsus. Not only is God's love antecedent to ours, but also it was borne in His heart toward us long before we were delivered from the power of darkness and translated into the Kingdom of His dear Son. It began not in time, but bears the date of eternity. "I have loved you with an everlasting love" (Jer 31:3).

"Herein is love, not that we loved God, but that He loved us, and sent His Son to be an atoning sacrifice for our sins' (1 John 4:10). It is clear from those words that God loved His people while they were in a state of nature, destitute of all grace, without a particle of love towards Him or faith in Him; yes, while they were His enemies (Rom 5:8,10). Clearly that lays me under a thousand times greater obligation to love, serve, and glorify Him than had He loved me for the first time when my heart was won. All the acts of God to His people in time, are the expressions of the love He bore them from eternity. It is because God loves us in Christ, and has done so from everlasting, that the gifts of His love are irrevocable. They are the bestowal of "the Father of lights, with whom is no variableness, neither shadow of turning." The love of God indeed makes a change in us when it is "shed abroad in our hearts," but it makes none in Him. He sometimes varies the dispensations of His providence toward us, but that is not because His affection has altered. Even when He chastens us, it is in love (Heb 12:6), since He has our good in view.

Let us look more closely at some of the operations of God's love. First, in election. "We are bound to give thanks always to God for you, brethren beloved of the Lord, because God has from the beginning chosen you to salvation through sanctification of the Spirit [His quickening] and belief of the truth" (2 Thess 2:13).

There is an infallible connection between God's love and His selection of those who were to be saved. That election is the consequence of His love is clear again from Deuteronomy: "The Lord did not set His love upon you, nor choose you, because you were more in number than any people" (7:7). So again: "In love, having predestinated us unto the adoption of children by Jesus Christ to Himself, according to the good pleasure of His will" (Eph 1:4,5).

Second, in redeeming. As we have seen from 1 John 4:10, out of His sovereign love God made provision for Christ to render satisfaction for their sins, though prior to their conversion He was angry with them in respect to His violated Law. And "how shall He not with Him also freely give us all things?" (Rom 8:32)—another clear proof that His Son was not "delivered up" to the cross for all mankind. For He gives them neither the Holy Spirit, a new nature, nor repentance and faith.

Third, effectual calling. From the enthroned Savior the Father sends forth the Holy Spirit (Acts 2:33). Having loved His elect with an everlasting love, with loving-kindness He draws them (Jer 31:3), quickens into newness of life, calls them out of darkness into His marvelous light, makes them His children. "Behold, what manner of love the Father has bestowed upon us, that we should be called the sons of God" (1 John 3:1). If filiation does not issue from God's love as a sure effect, to what purpose are those words?

Fourth, healing of backslidings: "I will heal their backsliding, I will love them freely" (Hosea 14:4), without reluctance or hesitation. "Many waters cannot quench love, neither can the floods drown it" (Song 8:7). Such is God's love to His people—invincible, unquenchable. Not only is there no possibility of its expiring, but also the black waters of backsliding cannot extinguish it, nor the floods of unbelief put it out.

Nothing is more irresistible in the natural world than death. In the realm of grace, nothing is so invincible as the love of God. Goodwin remarked: "What difficulties does the love of God overcome! For God to overcome His own heart! Do you think it was nothing for Him to put His Son to death? ... When He came to call us, had He no difficulties which love overcame? We were dead in trespasses and sins, yet from the great love wherewith He loved us, He quickened us in the grave of our corruption; even then did God come and conquer us. After our calling, how sadly do we provoke God! Such temptations that if it were possible the elect should be deceived. It is so with all Christians. No righteous man but he is scarcely saved (1 Peter 4:18), and yet saved he is, because the love of God is invincible—it overcomes all difficulties."

An application is hardly necessary for such a theme. Let God's love daily engage your mind by devout meditations on it so that the affections of your heart may be drawn out to Him.

When cast down in spirit, or in sore straits, plead His love in prayer, assured that it cannot deny anything good for you. Make God's wondrous love to you the incentive of your obedience to Him—gratitude requires nothing less.

CHAPTER 17
The Wrath of God

It is sad indeed to find so many professing Christians who appear to regard the wrath of God as something for which they need to make an apology, or who at least wish there were no such thing. While some who would not go so far as to openly admit that they consider it a blemish on the divine character, yet they are far from regarding it with delight; they do not like to think about it, and they rarely hear it mentioned without a secret resentment rising up in their hearts against it. Even with those who are more sober in their judgment, not a few seem to imagine that there is a severity about the divine wrath that makes it too terrifying to form a theme for profitable contemplation. Others harbor the delusion that God's wrath is not consistent with His goodness, and so seek to banish it from their thoughts.

Yes, many there are who turn away from a vision of God's wrath as though they were called to look upon some blotch in the divine character or some blot upon the divine government. But what says the Scriptures? As we turn to them we find that God has made no attempt to conceal the facts concerning His wrath. He is not ashamed to make it known that vengeance and fury belong unto Him. His own challenge is: "See now that I myself am He! There is no god besides Me. I put to death and I bring to life, I have wounded and I will heal, and no one can deliver out of my hand. I lift my hand to heaven and declare: As surely as I live forever, when I sharpen My flashing sword and My hand grasps it in judgment, I will take vengeance on My adversaries and repay those who hate Me" (Deut 32:39-41).

A study of the concordance will show that there are more references in Scripture to the anger, fury, and wrath of God—than there are to His love and tenderness. Because God is holy, He hates all sin; and because He hates all sin, His anger burns against the sinner. "God is angry with the wicked every day" (Psalm 7:11).

Now the wrath of God is as much a divine perfection as is His faithfulness, power, or mercy. It must be so, for there is no blemish whatever, not the slightest defect in the character of God; yet there would be if "wrath" were absent from Him! Indifference to sin is a moral blemish, and he who does not hate it, not is a moral leper. How could He who is the Sum of all excellency look with equal satisfaction upon virtue and vice, wisdom and folly? How could He who is infinitely holy disregard sin and refuse to manifest His "severity" (Rom 11:22) toward it? How could He, who delights only in that which is pure and lovely, not loathe and hate that which is impure and vile? The very nature of God makes Hell as real a necessity, as imperatively and eternally requisite, as Heaven is. Not only is there no imperfection in God, but there is no perfection in Him that is less perfect than another.

The wrath of God is His eternal detestation of all unrighteousness. It is the displeasure and indignation of divine equity against evil. It is the holiness of God stirred into activity against sin. It is the moving cause of that just sentence which He passes upon evildoers. God is angry against sin because it is a rebelling against His authority, a wrong done to His inviolable sovereignty. Insurrectionists against God's government shall be made to know that God is the Lord. They shall be made to feel how great that Majesty is which they despise, and how dreadful is that threatened wrath which they so little regarded. Not that God's anger is a malignant and malicious retaliation, inflicting injury for the sake of it, or in return for injury received. No, though God will vindicate His dominion as the Governor of the universe, He will not be vindictive.

That divine wrath is one of the perfections of God is not only evident from the considerations presented above, but is also clearly established by the express declarations of His own Word. "For the wrath of God is revealed from heaven" (Rom 1:18). Robert Haldane comments on this verse as follows: "It was revealed when the sentence of death was first pronounced, the earth cursed, and man driven out of the earthly paradise, and afterwards by such examples of punishment as those of the Deluge, and the destruction of the Cities of the Plain by fire from heaven; but especially by the reign of death throughout the world. It was proclaimed in the curse of the law on every transgression, and was intimated in the institution of sacrifice, and in all the services of the Mosaic dispensation. In the eighth chapter of this epistle, the Apostle calls the attention of believers to the fact that the whole creation has become subject to vanity, and groans and travails together in pain. The same creation which declares that there is a God, and publishes His glory, also proves that He is the Enemy of sin and the Avenger of the crimes of men...But above all, the wrath of God was revealed from heaven when the Son of God came down to manifest the divine character, and when that wrath was displayed in His sufferings and death, in a manner more awful than by all the tokens God had before given of His displeasure against sin. Besides this, the future and eternal punishment of the wicked is now declared in terms more solemn and explicit than formerly. Under the new dispensation, there are two revelations given from heaven—one of wrath, the other of grace."

Again, that the wrath of God is a divine perfection is plainly demonstrated by what we read in Psalm 95:11: "Unto whom I swore in My wrath." There are two occasions of God's "swearing": in making promises (Gen 22:16), and in pronouncing judgments (Deut 1:34ff). In the former, He swears in mercy to His children; in the latter, He swears to deprive a wicked generation of its inheritance because of murmuring and unbelief. An oath is for solemn confirmation (Heb 6:16). In Genesis 22:16 God says, "By Myself have I sworn." In Psalm 89:35 He declares, "Once have I sworn by My holiness." While in Psalm 95:11 He affirms, "I swear in My wrath." Thus the great Jehovah Himself appeals to His "wrath" as a perfection equal to His "holiness": He swears by the one as much as by the other! Again, as in Christ "dwells all the fullness of the Godhead bodily" (Col 2:9), and as all the divine perfections are illustriously displayed by Him (John 1:18), therefore do we read of "the wrath of the Lamb" (Rev 6:16).

The wrath of God is a perfection of the divine character upon which we need to frequently meditate.

First, that our hearts may be duly impressed by God's detestation of sin. We are ever prone to regard sin lightly, to gloss over its hideousness, to make excuses for it. But the more we study and ponder God's abhorrence of sin and His frightful vengeance upon it, the more likely are we to realize its heinousness.

Secondly, to beget a true fear in our souls for God: "Let us have grace whereby we may serve God acceptably with reverence and godly fear: for our God is a consuming fire" (Heb 12:28-29). We cannot serve him "acceptably" unless there is due "reverence" for His solemn Majesty and "godly fear" of His righteous anger; and these are best promoted by frequently calling to mind that "our God is a consuming fire."

Thirdly, to draw out our souls in fervent praise for our having been delivered from "the wrath to come" (1 Thess 1:10).

Our readiness or our reluctance to meditate upon the wrath of God becomes a sure test of our hearts' true attitude toward Him. If we do not truly rejoice in God, for what He is in Himself, and that because of all the perfections which are eternally resident in Him, then how dwells the love of God in us? Each of us needs to be most prayerfully on his guard against devising an image of God in our thoughts which is patterned after our own evil inclinations. Of old the Lord complained, "You thought that I was just like you" (Psalm 50:21). If we rejoice not "at the remembrance of His holiness" (Psalm 97:12), if we rejoice not to know that in a soon-coming Day, God will make a most glorious display of His wrath by taking vengeance upon all who now oppose Him, it is proof positive that our hearts are not in subjection to Him, that we are yet in our sins, and that we are on the way to the everlasting burnings.

"Rejoice, you nations, over His people, for He will avenge the blood of His servants. He will take vengeance on His adversaries; He will purify His land and His people" (Deut 32:43). And again we read—"After this I heard what sounded like the roar of a great multitude in heaven shouting—Hallelujah! Salvation and glory and power belong to our God, for true and just are His judgments. He has condemned the great prostitute who corrupted the earth by her adulteries. He has avenged on her the blood of his servants. And again they shouted—Hallelujah! The smoke from her goes up for ever and ever." (Rev 19:1-3).

Great will be the rejoicing of the saints in that day when the Lord shall vindicate His majesty, exercise His solemn dominion, magnify His justice, and overthrow the proud rebels who have dared to defy Him.

"If You, Lord, should mark iniquities, O Lord, who shall stand?" (Psalm 1303). Well may each of us ask this question, for it is written, "the ungodly shall not stand in the judgment" (Psalm 1:5). How sorely was Christ's soul exercised with thoughts of God's marking the iniquities of His people when they were upon Him! He was amazed and very heavy (Mark 14:33). His awful agony, His bloody sweat, His strong cries and supplications (Heb 5:7), His reiterated prayers ("If it is possible, let this cup pass from Me"), His last dreadful cry ("My God, My God, why have You forsaken Me?") all manifest what fearful apprehensions He had of what it was for God to "mark iniquities." Well may poor sinners cry out, "Lord, who shall stand," when the Son of God Himself so trembled beneath the weight of His wrath. If you, my reader, have not "fled for refuge" to Christ, the only Savior, "how will you do in the swelling of the Jordan?" (Jer 12:5).

"When I consider how the goodness of God is abused by the greatest part of mankind, I cannot but be of his mind that said—'The greatest miracle in the world is God's patience and bounty to an ungrateful world.' If a prince has an enemy surrounded in one of his towns, he does not send them in provisions, but lays close siege to the place, and does what he can to starve them. But the great God, who could wink all His enemies into destruction, bears with them, and is at daily cost to maintain them. Well may He command us to bless those who curse us, who Himself does good to the evil and unthankful. But think not, sinners, that you shall escape thus; God's mill goes slow, but grinds small, the more admirable His patience and bounty now is, the more dreadful and unsupportable will that fury be which arises out of His abused goodness. Nothing smoother than the sea, yet when stirred into a tempest, nothing rages more. Nothing so sweet as the patience and goodness of God, and nothing so terrible as His wrath when it takes fire" (William Gurnall, 1660).

Then "flee," my reader, flee to Christ; "flee from the wrath to come" (Matt 3:7) before it be too late. Do not, we earnestly beseech you, suppose that this message is intended for somebody else. It is to you! Do not be contented by thinking you have already fled to Christ. Make certain! Beg the Lord to search your heart and show you yourself.

A Word to Preachers—Brethren, do we in our teaching ministry, preach on this solemn subject as much as we ought? The Old Testament prophets frequently told their hearers that their wicked lives provoked the Holy One of Israel, and that they were treasuring up to themselves wrath against the day of wrath. And conditions in the world are no better now than they were then! Nothing is so calculated to arouse the careless and cause carnal professors to search their hearts, as to enlarge upon the fact that "God is angry with the wicked every day" (Psalm 7:11). The forerunner of Christ warned his hearers to "flee from the wrath to come" (Matt 3:7). The Savior bade His hearers, "Fear Him, who after He has killed, has power to cast into hell; yes, I say unto you, Fear Him" (Luke 12:5). The Apostle Paul said, "Knowing therefore the terror of the Lord, we persuade men" (2 Cor 5:11). Faithfulness demands that we speak as plainly about hell—as about heaven.

CHAPTER 18
The Contemplation of God

In the previous studies we have had in review some of the wondrous and lovely perfections of the divine character. From this most feeble and faulty contemplation of His attributes, it should be evident to us all that God is—

First, an incomprehensible Being, and, lost in wonder at His infinite greatness, we are constrained to adopt the words of Zophar, "Can you fathom the mysteries of God? Can you probe the limits of the Almighty? They are higher than the heavens—what can you do? They are deeper than the depths of the grave—what can you know? Their measure is longer than the earth and wider than the sea" (Job 11:7-9). When we turn our thoughts to God's eternity, His immateriality, His omnipresence, His almightiness, our minds are overwhelmed.

But the incomprehensibility of the divine nature is not a reason why we should desist from reverent inquiry and prayerful strivings to apprehend what He has so graciously revealed of Himself in His Word. Because we are unable to acquire perfect knowledge, it would be folly to say we will therefore make no efforts to attain to any degree of it. It has been well said: "Nothing will so enlarge the intellect, nothing so magnify the whole soul of man, as a devout, earnest, continued, investigation of the great subject of the Deity. The most excellent study for expanding the soul, is the science of Christ and Him crucified and the knowledge of the Godhead in the glorious Trinity" (C. H. Spurgeon).

Let us quote a little further from this prince of preachers: "The proper study of the Christian is the Godhead. The highest science, the loftiest speculation, the mightiest philosophy, which can engage the attention of a child of God is the name, the nature, the person, the doings, and the existence of the great God which he calls his Father. There is something exceedingly improving to the mind in a contemplation of the Divinity. It is a subject so vast, that all our thoughts are lost in its immensity; so deep, that our pride is drowned in its infinity. Other subjects we can comprehend and grapple with; in them we feel a kind of self-contentment, and go on our way with the thought, 'Behold I am wise.' But when we come to this master science, finding that our plumbline cannot sound its depth, and that our eagle eye cannot see its height, we turn away with the thought—I am but of yesterday and know nothing." (Sermon on Mal 3:6)

Yes, the incomprehensibility of the divine nature should teach us humility, caution, and reverence. After all our searchings and meditations we have to say with Job, "Lo, these are parts of His ways: but how little a portion is heard of Him?" (26:14). When Moses besought Jehovah for a sight of His glory, He answered him, "I will proclaim the name of the Lord before you" (Exo 33:19), and, as another has said: "The name is the collection of His attributes." Rightly did the Puritan John Howe declare: "The notion therefore we can hence form of His glory, is only such as we may have of a large volume by a brief synopsis; or of a spacious country by a little landscape. He has here given us a true report of Himself, but not a full account; such as will secure our apprehensions—being guided thereby from error, but not from ignorance. We can apply our minds to contemplate the several perfections whereby the blessed God discovers to us His being, and can in our thoughts attribute them all to Him, though we have still but low and defective conceptions of each one. Yet so far as our apprehensions can correspond to the discovery that He affords us of His several excellencies, we have a present view of His glory."

As the difference is indeed great between the knowledge of God which His saints have in this life—and that which they shall have in Heaven. Yet, as the former should not be undervalued because it is imperfect, so the latter is not to be magnified above its reality. True, the Scripture declare that we shall see "face to face" and "know" even as we are known (1 Cor 13:12). But to infer from this that we shall then know God as fully as He knows us, is to be misled by the mere sound of words, and to disregard the restriction of that knowledge that our finiteness necessarily requires. There is a vast difference between the saints being glorified—and their being made divine. In their glorified state, Christians will still be finite creatures, and therefore, never able to fully comprehend the infinite God.

"The saints in heaven will see God with the eye of the mind, for He will be always invisible to the bodily eye. They will see Him more clearly than they could see Him by reason and faith, and more extensively than all His works and dispensations had hitherto revealed Him. But their minds will not be so enlarged as to be capable of contemplating at once, or in detail, the whole excellence of His nature. To comprehend infinite perfection, they must become infinite themselves. Even in Heaven, their knowledge will be partial, but at the same time their happiness will be complete, because their knowledge will be perfect in this sense, that it will be adequate to the capacity of the subject, although it will not exhaust the fullness of the object. We believe that it will be progressive, and that as their views expand, their blessedness will increase. But it will never reach a limit beyond which there is nothing to be discovered, and when ages after ages have passed away, He will still be the incomprehensible God." (John Dick, 1840).

Secondly, from a review of the perfections of God, it appears that He is an all-sufficient Being. He is all-sufficient in Himself and to Himself. As the First of beings, He could receive nothing from another, nor be limited by the power of another. Being infinite, He is possessed of all possible perfection. When the Triune God existed all alone, He was all to Himself. His understanding, His love, His energies, found an adequate object in Himself. Had He stood in need of anything external He would not have been independent, and therefore He would not have been God. He created all things, and that for Himself (Col 1:16), yet it was not in order to supply a lack—but that He might communicate life and happiness to angels and men, and admit them to the vision of His glory. True, He demands the allegiance and services of His intelligent creatures, yet He derives no benefit from their offices; all the advantage redounds to themselves (Job 22:2-3). He makes use of means and instruments to accomplish His ends, yet not from a deficiency of power, but oftentimes to more strikingly display His power through the feebleness of the instruments.

The all-sufficiency of God, makes Him to be the Supreme Object which is ever to be sought unto. True happiness consists only in the enjoyment of God. His favor is life, and His loving-kindness is better than life. "The Lord is my portion, says my soul; therefore will I hope in Him" (Lam 3:24). His love, His grace, and His glory are the chief objects of the saints' desire and the springs of their highest satisfaction.

"Many are asking—Who can show us any good? Let the light of your face shine upon us, O Lord. You have filled my heart with greater joy than when their grain and new wine abound." (Psalm 4:6,7).
Yes, the Christian, when in his right mind, is able to say: "Even though the fig trees have no blossoms, and there are no grapes on the vine; even though the olive crop fails, and the fields lie empty and barren; even though the

flocks die in the fields, and the cattle barns are empty, yet I will rejoice in the Lord! I will be joyful in the God of my salvation." (Hab 3:17,18).

Thirdly, from a review of the perfections of God, it appears that He is the Supreme Sovereign of the universe. It has been rightly said: "No dominion is so absolute as that which is founded on creation. He who might not have made anything, had a right to make all things according to His own pleasure. In the exercise of His uncontrolled power, He has made some parts of the creation mere inanimate matter, of grosser or more refined texture, and distinguished by different qualities, but all inert and unconscious. He has given organization to other parts, and made them susceptible of growth and expansion, but still without life in the proper sense of the term. To others He has given not only organization, but conscious existence, organs of sense and self-motive power. To these He has added in man the gift of reason, and an immortal spirit, by which he is allied to a higher order of beings who are placed in the superior regions. Over the world which He has created, He sways the scepter of omnipotence. 'At the end of that time, I, Nebuchadnezzar, raised my eyes toward heaven, and my sanity was restored. Then I praised the Most High; I honored and glorified him who lives forever. His dominion is an eternal dominion; his kingdom endures from generation to generation. All the peoples of the earth are regarded as nothing. He does as he pleases with the powers of heaven and the peoples of the earth. No one can hold back his hand or say to him-What have you done?' Daniel 4:34-35" (John Dick).

A creature, considered as such, has no rights. He can demand nothing from his Maker; and in whatever manner he may be treated, has no title to complain. Yet, when thinking of the absolute dominion of God over all, we ought never to lose sight of His moral perfections. God is just and good, and ever does that which is right. Nevertheless, He exercises His sovereignty according to His own imperial and righteous pleasure. He assigns each creature his place as seems good in His own sight. He orders the varied circumstances of each according to His own counsels. He molds each vessel according to His own uninfluenced determination. He has mercy on whom He will, and He hardens whom He will. Wherever we are, His eye is upon us. Whoever we are, our life and everything is held at His disposal. To the Christian, He is a tender Father; to the rebellious sinner He will yet be a consuming fire. "Now unto the King eternal, immortal, invisible, the only wise God, be honor and glory forever and ever. Amen" (1 Tim 1:17).

CHAPTER 19
The Bounties of God

"Eye has not seen, nor ear heard, neither have entered into the heart of man—the things which God has prepared for those who love him" (1 Cor. 2:9). How often this passage is quoted only that far; how rarely are the words added, "But God has revealed them unto us by his Spirit" (verse 10). Why is this? Is it because so few of God's people search out and enjoy what the Spirit has revealed in the Word about those things which God has prepared for those who love Him? If we were more occupied with God's riches than with our poverty, Christ's fullness than our emptiness, the divine bounties than our leanness—on what a different level of experience we would live!

We are much impressed by noting some of "the riches of His grace" (Eph. 1:7). It is striking to note that our Christian life starts at a marriage feast (Luke 14:16-23; Matthew 2-10), just as Christ's first miracle was wrought at one (John 2). The word to us is, "Come, for all things are now ready" (Luke 14:17); "Behold, I have prepared my dinner: my oxen and my fatlings are killed, and all things are ready; come unto the marriage" (Matthew 22:4). Observe the "I have prepared," agreeing with "the things which God has prepared for them that love Him" (1 Cor. 2:9). Notice the "are ready," confirming "God has revealed them unto us" (1 Cor. 2:10). Mark the "my dinner, my oxen and my fatlings," for "all things are of God" (2 Cor. 5:18). The creature contributes nothing; all is provided for him. Finally, weigh the "come unto the marriage." The figure is very blessed; it speaks of joy, festivity, feasting.

He spread the banquet, made me eat.
Bid all my fears remove,
Yes, o'er my guilty, rebel head
He placed His banner—Love.

Practically the same figure is employed by Christ again in Luke 15. There He pictures the penitent prodigal welcomed home by the father. No sooner is he clothed and fitted for the house than the words go forth, "Bring hither the fattened calf, and kill it; and let us eat, and be merry" (verse 23); and we are told "they began to be merry." In the parable, that merriment met with no reverse, since it is portrayed without a break and without a bound. Then we may conclude that this newborn joy ought to characterize all this festive scene—as truly so now, as soon it will be in glory.

A beautiful type of the lavish manner in which God bestows His bounties upon His people is found in Genesis 9:3: "Every moving thing that lives shall be food for you; even as the green herb have I given you all things." This was Jehovah's response to the "sweet savor" which He had just smelled. It is most important that we should note the connection, and perceive the ground on which God so freely bestowed "all things" upon the patriarch. At the close of Genesis 8 Noah built an altar unto the Lord, and presented burnt offerings. At the beginning of Genesis 9 we learn God's answer, which blessedly foreshadowed the unmeasured portion bestowed upon the new creation, the members of which have been blessed "with all spiritual blessings in heavenly places in Christ" (Eph. 1:3).

These blessings are based upon God's estimate of the value of Christ's sacrifice of Himself. The abiding worth of that sacrifice is immeasurable and illimitable, as immeasurable as the personal excellency of the Son, as illimitable as the Father's delight in Him. The nature and extent of those blessings, which accrue to God's elect on the ground of Christ's finished work, are intimated by the substantives and adjectives employed by the Holy Spirit when He describes the profuseness of the divine bounties already bestowed upon us, and which we shall enjoy forever!

Take first God's grace. Not only are we told of the "riches of his grace" (Eph. 1:7), and of the "exceeding riches of His grace" (Eph. 2:7), but also we read that it has "abounded unto many," and that we receive "abundance of grace," yes, that grace has super-abounded (Romans 5:15, 17, 20)—the limitless wealth of divine grace flowing forth and multiplying itself in its objects. The foundation or moving cause of this is found in John 1. When the only begotten Son became flesh and tabernacled here for a season, it was as One who was "full of grace and truth." Because we have been made joint heirs with Him it is written, "And of his fullness have all we received, and grace for grace" (verse 16).

Take again God's love. There has been neither reserve nor restraint in the outflow of His love to its loveless, unlovely objects. He has loved His people with an everlasting love (Jer. 31:3). Wondrously He manifested it, for when the fullness of time was come, He sent forth His Son, born of a woman. Yes,

He did so love the world as to give His only begotten Son, "that whoever believes in him should not perish, but have everlasting life": therefore we read of His "great love wherewith he loved us" (Eph. 2:4). The Greek word translated "great" is rendered "plenteous" (Matthew 9:37), and "abundant" (1 Pet. 1:3). Love unmeasured, which passes knowledge, fills our lives with its unceasing ministrations, ever active in priesthood and advocacy on high, how truly it is love abundant.

Our present theme is inexhaustible. Our Lord came here that His people "might have life, and that they might have it more abundantly" (John 10:10). This was first made good when Christ, as the Head of the new creation and the "beginning of the creation of God" (Rev. 3:14), breathed on His disciples, "Receive the Holy Spirit." It was the risen Savior communicating His resurrection life to His own (compare Genesis 2:7 for the beginning of the old creation). So too when that same One, who down here received the Spirit without measure (John 3:34), ascended on high as the glorified Man, He baptized His people in the Holy Spirit (Acts 2). As the apostle Paul assures Gentile saints, "He shed on us abundantly" (Titus 3:6). Once more, he emphasized the profuseness of God's bounties.

Consider now His confidences. The Lord Jesus said to His disciples, "Henceforth I call you not servants; for the servant knows not what his Lord does: but I have called you friends; for all things that I have heard of my Father I have made known unto you" (John 15:15). There are things which the angels "desire to look into" (1 Pet. 1:12), yet they have been made known to us by God's Spirit. What a word in Ephesians, "Wherein he has abounded toward us in all wisdom and prudence; having made known unto us the mystery of his will" (Eph. 1:8-9) This may be termed the abundance of His counsels.

Once more, consider the exercise and display of His power. Paul prayed that we might know, "the incredible greatness of his power for us who believe him. This is the same mighty power that raised Christ from the dead and seated him in the place of honor at God's right hand in the heavenly realms" (Eph. 1:19-20). Here was the might of God working transcendently in an objective way; its correlative is recorded in Ephesians 3:20: "Now unto him that is able to do exceeding abundantly above all that we ask or think, according to the power that works in us." Clearly this is the highest putting forth of energy, working subjectively.

In such lavish measure then God has blessed His people. As the apostle wrote to the Colossians concerning Him, "For in him dwells all the fullness of the Godhead bodily. And you are complete [filled full] in him" (Col. 2:9-10). But it is one thing to know, intellectually, of these bounties of God; it is quite another, by faith, to make them our own. It is one thing to be familiar with the letter of them; it is another to live in their power and be the personal expression of them.

What shall our response be to such divine munificence? Surely it is that "the abundant grace might through the thanksgiving of many redound to the glory of God" (2 Cor. 4:15). Surely it is that we should "abound in hope, through the power of the Holy Spirit" (Romans 15:13). It is only here that hope finds its sphere of exercise, since only in the saints will it receive full fruition. If God speaks so uniformly of the varied character of our blessing—whether it be His grace, His love, His life imparted to us, His confidences, His power, His mercy (1 Pet. 1:3 ff.)—as being so abundant, it must be because He wants to impress our hearts with the exuberance of the bounties He has bestowed on us. The practical effect of this on our souls should cause us to "rejoice in God through our Lord Jesus Christ" (Romans 5:11), to draw out all that is within us in true worship, to fit us for a closer and deeper fellowship with Him. "And God is able to make all grace abound toward you; that you, always having all sufficiency in all things, may abound to every good work" (2 Cor. 9:8).

CHAPTER 20
The Gifts of God

A GIVING GOD! What a concept! To our regret, our familiarity with it often dulls our sense of wonderment at it. There is nothing that resembles such a concept in the religions of heathendom. Very much to the contrary; their deities are portrayed as monsters of cruelty and greed, always exacting painful sacrifices from deluded devotees. But the God of Scripture is portrayed as the Father of mercies, "who gives us richly all things to enjoy" (1 Tim. 6:17). It is true that: He has His own rights—the rights of His holiness and proprietorship. Nor does He rescind them, but rather enforces them. But what we would contemplate here is something which transcends reason and had never entered our minds to conceive. The Divine Claimer is at once the Divine Meeter. He required satisfaction of His broken Law, and Himself supplied it. His just claims are met by His own grace. He who asks for sacrifices from us—made the supreme sacrifice for us! God is both the Demander and the Donor, the Requirer and the Provider.

1. The gift of His Son. Of old the language of prophecy announced: "For unto us a child is born, unto us a son is given" (Isaiah 9:6). Accordingly, the angels announced to the shepherds at the time of His advent: "Unto you is born this day . . . a Savior" (Luke 2:11). That gift was the supreme exemplification of the divine benignity. "God showed how much he loved us by sending his only Son into the world so that we might have eternal life through him. This is real love. It is not that we loved God, but that he loved us and sent his Son as a sacrifice to take away our sins" (1 John 4:9-10). That was the guaranty of all other blessings. As the apostle argued from the greater to the less, assuring us that Christ is at once the pledge and channel of every other mercy: "He who spared not his own Son, but delivered him up for us all, how shall he not with him also freely give us all things?" (Romans 8:32). God did not withhold His choicest treasure, the darling of His bosom, but freely yielded Him up; and the love which did not spare Him, will not begrudge anything that is for the good of His people.

2. The gift of His Spirit. The Son is God's all-inclusive gift. As Manton said, "Christ comes not to us empty handed: His person and His benefits are not divided. He came to purchase all manner of blessings for us." The greatest of these is the Holy Spirit, who applies and communicates what the Lord Jesus obtained for His people. God pardoned and justified His elect in Old Testament times on the ground of the atonement, which His Son would make at the appointed time. On the same basis He communicated to them the Spirit (Num. 9:25; Nehemiah 9:20), otherwise none would have been regenerated, fitted for communion with God, or enabled to bring forth spiritual fruit. But He then wrought more secretly, rather than "in demonstration and in power"; came as "the dew," rather than was "poured out" copiously; was restricted to Israel, rather than communicated to Gentiles also. The Spirit in His fullness was God's ascension gift to Christ (Acts 2:33) and Christ's coronation gift to His Church (John 16:7). The gift of the Spirit was purchased for His people by Christ (see Galatians 3:13-14 and note carefully the second "that" in verse 14). Every blessing we receive is through the merits and mediation of Christ.

    3. The gift of eternal life. "For the wages of sin is death, but the gift of God is eternal life through Jesus Christ our Lord" (Romans 6:23). There is a double antithesis between those two things. First, the justice of God will render unto the wicked what is due them for their sins; but His mercy bestows upon His people what they do not deserve. Second, eternal death follows as a natural and inevitable consequence from what is in and done by its objects. Not so eternal life, for it is bestowed without any consideration of something in or from its subjects. It is communicated and sustained gratuitously. Eternal life is a free bounty, not only unmerited but also unsolicited by us, for in every instance God has reason to say, "I am found by those who sought me not" (Isaiah 65:1; cf. Romans 3:11). The recipient is wholly passive. He does not act, but is acted upon when he is brought from death unto life. Eternal life—a spiritual life now, a life of glory hereafter—is sovereignly and freely bestowed by God. Yet it is also a blessing communicated by Him unto His elect because the Lord Jesus Christ paid the price of redemption. Yes, it is actually dispensed by Christ. "I give unto them [not merely "offer"] eternal life" (John 10:28; see also 17:3).

    4. The gift of spiritual understanding. "And we know that the Son of God has come, and has given us an understanding, that we may know him that is true" (1 John 5:20). What is communicated to the saint when he is born again is wholly spiritual and exactly suited for taking in the Scriptural knowledge of Christ. It is not an entirely new faculty which is then imparted, but rather the renewing of the original one, fitting it for the apprehension of new objects. It consists of an internal illumination, a divine light that shines in our hearts, enabling us to discern the glory of God shining in the face of Jesus Christ (2 Cor. 4:6). Though we are not now admitted into a corporeal sight of Christ, yet He is made a living reality to those who have been quickened into newness of life. By this divine renewing of the understanding we can now perceive the peerless excellency and perfect suitability of Christ. The knowledge we have of Him is seated in the understanding. That fires the affections, sanctifies the will, and raises the mind into being fixed upon Him. Such a spiritual understanding is not attained by any efforts of ours, but is a supernatural bestowment, a divine gift conferred upon the elect, which admits them into the secrets of the Most High.

5. The gift of faith. The salvation of God does not actually become ours until we believe in, rest upon, and receive Christ as a personal Savior. But as we cannot see without both sight and light, neither can we believe until life and faith are divinely communicated to us. Accordingly, "For by grace are you saved through faith; and that not of yourselves: it is the gift of God: not of works, lest any man should boast" (Eph. 2:8-9). Arminians would make the second clause of verse 8 a mere repetition of the first, and in less expressive and emphatic language. Since salvation is by grace, it is superfluous to add that it is "not of yourselves." But because "faith" is our act, it was necessary—so that the excellency of it should not be arrogated by the creature, but ascribed unto God—to point out that faith is not of ourselves. The very faith which receives a gratuitous salvation is not the unassisted act of man's own will. As God must give me breath before I can breathe, so faith before I believe. Compare also "faith which is by him" (Acts 3:16); "who believe, according to the working of his mighty power" (Eph. 1:19); "through the faith of the operation of God" (Col. 2:12); "who by him do believe in God" (1 Pet. 1:21).

6. The gift of repentance. While it is the bound duty of every sinner to repent (Acts 17:30)—for ought he not to cease from and abhor his rebellion against God?—yet he is so completely under the blinding power of sin that a miracle of grace is necessary before he will do so. A broken and a contrite spirit are of God's providing. It is the Holy Spirit who illuminates the understanding to perceive the heinousness of sin, the heart to loathe it, and the will to repudiate it. Faith and repentance are the first evidence of spiritual life. For when God quickens a sinner He convicts him of the evil of sin, causes him to hate it, moves him to sorrow over and turn from it. "After I strayed, I repented; after I came to understand, I beat my breast. I was ashamed and humiliated because I bore the disgrace of my youth." (Jer. 31:19). "A Prince and a Savior—to give repentance to Israel" (Acts 5:31); "Then has God also to the Gentiles granted repentance unto life" (Acts 11:18); "if God perhaps will give them repentance" (2 Tim. 2:25).

7. The gift of grace. "I thank my God always on your behalf, for the grace of God which is given you by Jesus Christ" (1 Cor. 1:4). Grace is used there in its widest sense, including all the benefits of Christ's merits and mediation, providential or spiritual, temporal or eternal. It includes regenerating, sanctifying, preserving grace, as well as every particular grace of the new nature—faith, hope, love. "But unto every one of us, is given grace according to the measure of the gift of Christ" (Eph. 4:7), that is, according as He is pleased to bestow, and not according to our ability or asking. Therefore we have no cause to be proud or boastful. Whatever grace we have to resist the devil, patiently bear affliction, or overcome the world—is from Him. Whatever obedience we perform, or devotion we render Him, or sacrifice we make—is of His grace. Therefore must we confess, "for all things come of you, and of your own have we given you" (1 Chron. 29:14).

CHAPTER 21
The Guidance of God

There is a need to amplify the positive aspect of divine guidance. There are few subjects which bear on the practical side of the Christian life, and that believers are more exercised about, than that they may be "led of the Lord" in all their ways. Yet when some important decision has to be made, they are often puzzled to know how "the Lord's mind" is obtained. Great numbers of tracts and booklets on this subject have been written, but they are so vague that they offer little help. There certainly exists a real need today for some clear, definitive treatment of the subject.

For some years I have been convinced that one thing which contributes much to shrouding this subject in mystery is the loose, misleading terms generally employed by those who refer to it. While such expressions are used, "Is this according to God's will?", "Do I have the prompting of the Holy Spirit?", "Were you led of the Lord in that?", sincere minds will continue to be perplexed and never arrive at any certainty. These expressions are so commonly used in religious circles that probably quite a few readers will be surprised at our challenging them. We certainly do not condemn these expressions as erroneous, but rather we wish to point out that they are too intangible for most people until more definitely defined.

What alternative, then, have we to suggest? In connection with every decision we make, every plan we form, every action we execute, let the question be, "Is this in harmony with God's Word?" Is it what the Scriptures enjoin? Does it square with the rule God has given us to walk by? Is it in accord with the example which Christ left us to follow? If it is in harmony with God's Word, then it must be "according to God's will," for His will is revealed in His Word. If I do what the Scriptures enjoin, then I must be "prompted by the Holy Spirit," for He never moves anyone to act contrary thereto. If my conduct squares with the rule of righteousness (the precepts and commands of the Word), then I must be "led of the Lord," for He leads only into the "paths of righteousness" (Psalm 23:1, 3). A great deal of mystical vagueness and puzzling uncertainty will be removed if the reader substitutes for, "Is this according to God's will?" the simpler and more tangible, "Is this according to God's Word?"

God, in His infinite condescension and transcendent grace, has given us His Word for this very purpose, so that we need not stumble along blindly, ignorant of what pleases or displeases Him—but that we might know His mind. That divine Word is given to us not simply for information, but to regulate our conduct, to enlighten our minds, and to mold our hearts. The Word supplies us with an unerring chart by which to steer through the dangerous sea of life. If we sincerely and diligently follow, it will deliver us from disastrous rocks and submerged reefs, and direct us safely to the heavenly harbor. That Word has all the instructions we need for every problem, every emergency we may be called upon to face. That Word has been given to us "that the man of God may be perfect, thoroughly furnished unto all good works" (2 Tim. 3:17). How thankful we should be that the Triune God has favored us with such a Word.

"Your word is a lamp unto my feet, and a light unto my path" (Psalm 119:105). The metaphor used here is taken from a man walking along a dangerous road on a dark night, in urgent need of a lantern to show him where to walk safely and comfortably, to avoid injury and destruction. The same figure is used again in the New Testament. "We have also a more sure word of prophecy; whereunto you do well that you take heed, as unto a light that shines in a dark place" (2 Pet. 1:19). The dark place is this world, and it is only as we take heed to the Word, to the light God has given us, that we shall be able to perceive and avoid "the broad road which leads to destruction," and discern the narrow way which alone "leads unto Life."

It should be observed that this verse plainly intimates God has placed His Word in our hands for an intensely practical purpose, namely, to direct our walk and to regulate our deportment. At once this shows us what is the first and principal use we are to make of this divine gift. It would do a traveler little good to diligently scrutinize the mechanism of a lamp, or to admire its beautiful design. Rather he is to take it up and make a practical use of it. Many are zealous in reading "the letter of Scripture," and many are charmed with the evidences of its divine Authorship. But how few realize the primary purpose for which God gave the Scriptures, how few make a practical use of them—ordering the details of their lives by its rules and regulations. They eulogize the lamp, but they do not walk by its light.

Our first need as little children was to learn to walk. The mother's milk was only a means to an end: to nourish the infant's life, to strengthen its limbs so that they should be put to a practical use. So it is spiritually. When we have been born again and fed by the Spirit on the pure milk of the Word, our first need is to learn to walk, to walk as the children of God. This can be learned only as we ascertain our Father's will as revealed in Holy Writ. By nature we are totally ignorant of His will for us and of what promotes our highest interests. It is solemn and humbling that man is the only creature born into this world devoid of intelligence as to how to act, and who needs to be taught what is evil and what is good for him.

All the lower orders of creation are endowed with an instinct which moves them to act discreetly, to avoid what is harmful, and to follow what is good. But not so man. Animals and birds do not have to be taught which herbs and berries are poisonous; they need no curbs upon them not to overeat or over drink—you cannot even force a horse or a cow to gorge and make itself sick. Even plants turn their faces to the light and open their mouths to catch the falling rain. But fallen man has not even the instinct of the brutes! Usually he has to learn by painful experience what is harmful and injurious. And, as it has been well said, "Experience keeps an expensive school"—her fees are high. Too bad that so many only discover this when it is too late, when they have wrecked their constitutions beyond repair.

Some may answer to this, "But man is endowed with a conscience." True, but how well does it serve him until he is enlightened by the Word and convicted by the Spirit? Man's understanding has been so darkened by sin, and folly is so bound up in his heart from childhood (Proverbs 22:15), that until he is instructed he does not know what God requires of him, nor what is for his highest good. That is why God gave us His Word: to make known what He justly demands of us; to inform us of those things which destroy the soul; to reveal the baits which Satan uses to capture and slay so many; to point out the highway of holiness which alone leads to heaven (Heb. 12:14); and to acquaint us with the rules which must be observed if we are to walk that highway.

Our first duty, and our first aim, must be to take up the Scriptures to ascertain what is God's revealed will for us, what are the paths He forbids us to walk, what are the ways pleasing in His sight. Many things are prohibited in the Word which neither our reason nor our conscience would discover. For example, we learn, "that which is highly esteemed among men is abomination in the sight of God" (Luke 16:15); "the friendship of the world is enmity with God" (James 4:4); "he who hastens with his feet sins" (Proverbs 19:2). Many things are also commanded which can only be known if we acquaint ourselves with its contents. For example, "Lean not unto your own understanding" (Proverbs 3:5); "Put not your trust in princes, nor in man, in whom there is no help" (Psalm 146:3); "Love your enemies, bless those who curse you, do good to those who hate you, and pray for those who despitefully use you and persecute you" (Matthew 5:44).

The above are but samples of hundreds of others. It is obvious that God's Word cannot be a lamp unto our feet and a light unto our path unless we are familiar with its contents, particularly until we are informed on the practical rules God has given us to walk by. Hence it should be obvious that the first need of the Christian is not to delve into the intricacies and mysteries of Scripture, study the prophecies, nor entertain himself with the wonderful types therein. Rather he needs to concentrate on what will instruct him as to the kind of conduct which will be pleasing to the Lord. The Scriptures are given us, primarily, not for our intellectual gratification, nor for emotional admiration, but for life's regulation. Nor are the precepts and commands, the warnings and encouragements contained therein simply for our information. They are to be reduced to practice, they require unqualified obedience.

"Do not let this Book of the Law depart from your mouth; meditate on it day and night, so that you may be careful to do everything written in it. Then you will be prosperous and successful" (Josh. 1:8). God will be no man's debtor. In keeping His commands there is "great reward" (Psalm 19:11). Part of that reward is deliverance from being deceived by the false appearances of things, from forming erroneous estimates, from pursuing a foolish policy. Part of that reward is acquiring wisdom so that we choose what is good, act prudently, and follow those paths which lead to righteousness, peace, and joy. He who treasures the divine precepts in his heart, and diligently seeks to walk by their rule, will escape those evils which destroy his fellows.

"If any man walks in the day, he stumbles not, because he sees the light of this world" (John 11:9). To walk in the day means to be in communion with One who is Light, to conduct ourselves according to His revealed will. Just so far as the Christian walks in the path of duty, as defined for him in the Word, will he walk surely and comfortably. The light of that Word makes the way plain before him, and he is preserved from falling over the obstacles with which Satan seeks to trip him. "But if a man walk in the night, he stumbles, because there is no light in him" (verse 10). Here is the solemn contrast: he who walks according to the dictates of his lusts and follows the counsel and example of the ungodly, falls into the snares of the devil, and perishes. There is no light in such an one, for he is not regulated by the Sun of righteousness.

"I am the light of the world: he who follows me shall not walk in darkness, but shall have the light of life" (John 8:12). It is one thing to have "life," it is another to enjoy the "light of life" that is only obtained by following Christ. Notice the tense of the verb: it is "he who follows me," which signifies a steady, continuous course of action. The promise to such a one is, "he shall not walk in darkness." But what does it mean to follow Christ? First and foremost, to be emptied of self-will, for "even Christ pleased not himself" (Romans 15:3). It is absolutely essential that self-will and self-pleasing be mortified, if we are to be delivered from walking in darkness.

The unchanging order is made known by Christ, "If any man will come after me, let him deny himself, and take up his cross, and follow me" (Matthew 16:24). Christ cannot be followed until self is denied and the cross accepted as the distinguishing mark of discipleship. What does it mean to deny self? It means to repudiate our own goodness, to renounce our own wisdom, to have no confidence in our own strength, to completely set aside our own will and wishes, that we should not hence forth live unto ourselves, but unto Him who died for us (2 Cor. 5:15). What does it mean to "take up our cross"? It signifies a readiness to endure the world's hatred and scorn, to voluntarily surrender our lives to God, to use all our faculties for His glory. The cross stands for unreserved and loving obedience to the Lord, for of Him it is written, that "He became obedient unto death, even the death of the cross." It is only as self with all its lustings and interests is denied, and as the heart is dominated by the spirit of Calvary, that we are prepared to follow Christ.

And what is signified by "follow" Christ? It means to take His yoke upon us (Matthew 11:29), and live in complete subjection to Him; to yield fully to His Lordship, to obey His commands, and thus truly serve Him. It is seeking to do only those things which are pleasing in His sight; to emulate the example which He left us—and He was subject to the Scriptures in all things. As we follow Him, we "shall not walk in darkness." We will be in happy fellowship with Him who is the true light. For our encouragement for they were men of like passions—it is recorded of Caleb and Joshua, "they have wholly followed the Lord" (Num. 32:12). Having put their hand to the plow, they did not look back. Consequently, instead of perishing in the wilderness with their disobedient fellows, they entered the promised land.

Thus the great business, the task of the Christian, is to regulate his life by and conform his conduct to the precepts of the written Word and the example left us by the Incarnate Word. As he does so, and in proportion as he does so, he is emancipated from the darkness of his natural mind, freed from the follies of his corrupt heart, delivered from the mad course of this world, and he escapes the snares of the devil. "Through knowledge shall the just be delivered" (Proverbs 11:9). Yes, great is the reward of keeping God's commandments. "Then shall you understand righteousness, and judgment, and equity; yes, every good path. When wisdom enters into your heart, and knowledge is pleasant unto your soul; discretion shall preserve you, understanding shall keep you" (Proverbs 2:9-11).

It is well for those who are sensitive to both their own weakness and fallibility, and the difficulties with which they are surrounded in life, that the Lord has promised to guide His people with His eye, to cause them to hear, "This is the way—walk in it," when they are in danger of turning aside. For this purpose He has given to us the written Word as a lamp to our feet, and encourages us to pray for the teaching of His Holy Spirit so that we may rightly understand and apply it. However, too often many widely deviate from the path of duty and commit gross, perplexing mistakes, while they profess a sincere desire to know the will of God, and think they have His warrant and authority. This must certainly be due to misapplication of the rule by which they judge, since the rule itself is infallible. The Scriptures cannot deceive us, if rightly understood; but they may, if perverted, confirm us in a mistake. The Holy Spirit cannot mislead those under His influence; but we may suppose that we are so, when we are not.

Many have been deceived as to what they ought to do, or into forming a judgment beforehand of events in which they are closely concerned, by expecting direction in ways which the Lord has not warranted. Here are some of the principal ones:

Some, when two or more things were in view, and they could not immediately determine which to prefer, committed their case to the Lord in prayer. Then they have proceeded to cast lots, taking it for granted, after such a solemn appeal, that the turning up of the lot might be safely rested on as an answer from God. It is true, the Scripture (and right reason) assures us that the Lord disposes the lot. Several cases are recorded in the Old Testament where lots were used by divine appointment. But I think neither these, nor the choosing of Matthias to the apostleship by lot, are proper precedents for our conduct. In the division of the land of Canaan, in the affair of Achan, and in the nomination of Saul to the kingdom, recourse to lots was by God's express command. The instance of Matthias likewise was singular, since it can never happen again (namely, the choice of an apostle).

All these were before the canon of Scripture was completed, and before the full descent and communication of the Holy Spirit, who was promised to dwell with the Church to the end of time. Under the New Testament dispensation, we are invited to come boldly to the throne of grace, to make our request known to the Lord, and to cast our cares upon Him. But we have neither precept nor promise respecting the use of lots. To have recourse to them without His appointment seems to be tempting Him rather than honoring Him, and it savors more of presumption than dependence. Effects of this expedient have often been unhappy and hurtful, a sufficient proof of how little it is to be trusted as a guide of our conduct.

Others, when in doubt, have opened the Bible and expected to find something to direct them to the first verse they should cast their eye upon. It is no small discredit to this practice that the heathens used some of their favorite books in the same way. They based their persuasions of what they ought to do, or what would befall them, according to the passage they happened upon. Among the Romans, the writings of Virgil were frequently consulted on these occasions. Indeed, Virgil is as well adapted to satisfy inquiries in this way as the Bible itself. For if people will be governed by the occurrence of a single text of Scripture without regarding the context, or comparing it with the general tenor of the Word and with their own circumstances, they may commit the greatest extravagances. They may expect the greatest impossibilities, and contradict the plainest dictates of common sense, and all the while they think they have the Word of God on their side. Can opening to 2 Samuel 7:3, when Nathan said unto David, "Do all that is in your heart, for the Lord is with you," be sufficient to determine the lawfulness or expediency of actions? Or can a glance of the eye upon our Lord's words to the woman of Canaan, "Be it unto you even as you will" (Matthew 15:28), amount to proof that the present earnest desire of the mind (whatever it may be) shall be surely accomplished? Yet it is certain that big matters with important consequences have been engaged in, and the most optimistic expectations formed, upon no better warrant than dipping (as it is called) upon a text of Scripture.

A sudden strong impression of a text that seems to have some resemblance to the concern on the mind has been accepted by many as an infallible token that they were right, and that things would go just as they would have them. Or, on the other hand, if the passage bore a threatening aspect—it has filled them with fears which they have found afterwards were groundless. These impressions have been more generally regarded and trusted to, but have frequently proved no less delusive. It is true that such impressions of a precept or a promise that humble, animate, or comfort the soul, by giving it a lively sense of the truth contained in the words, are both profitable and pleasant. Many of the Lord's people have been instructed and supported (especially in a time of trouble) by some seasonable word of grace applied and sealed by His Spirit to their hearts. But if impressions or impulses are received as a voice from heaven, directing to particular actions that could not be proved to be duties without them, a person may be inwardly misled into great evils and gross delusions. Many have been so. There is no doubt that the enemy of our souls, if permitted, can furnish us with Scriptures in abundance for these purposes.

Some people judge of the nature and event of their designs by the freedom they find in prayer. They say that they commit their ways to God, seek His direction, and are favored with much enlargement of spirit. Therefore they cannot doubt but what they have in view is acceptable in the Lord's sight. I would not absolutely reject every plea of this kind, yet without other corroborating evidence I could not admit it as proof. It is not always easy to determine when we have spiritual freedom in prayer. Self is deceitful. When our hearts are much fixed upon a thing, this may put words and earnestness into our mouths. Too often we first determine secretly for ourselves, and then ask counsel of God. In such a disposition we are ready to grasp at everything that may seem to favor our darling scheme. And the Lord, for the detecting and chastisement of our hypocrisy (for hypocrisy it is, though perhaps hardly perceptible to ourselves), may answer us according to our idols (see Ezekiel 14:3-4).

Besides, the grace of prayer may be in exercise when the subject matter of the prayer may be founded upon a mistake, from the intervention of circumstances with which we are unacquainted. Thus, I may have a friend in a distant country. I hope he is alive, I pray for him, and it is my duty to do so. The Lord, by His Spirit, assists His people in their present duty. If I can pray with much liberty for my distant friend, it may be a proof that the Spirit is pleased to assist my infirmities, but it is no proof my friend is alive at the time I pray for him. If the next time I pray for him I should find my spirit straitened, I am not to conclude that my friend is dead, and therefore the Lord will not assist me in praying for him any longer.

Once more, a remarkable dream has often been thought as decisive as any of these methods of knowing the will of God. True, many wholesome and seasonable admonitions have been received in dreams. But to pay great attention to dreams, or especially to be guided by them, to form our sentiments, conduct our expectations upon them—is superstitious and dangerous. The promises are not made to those who dream, but to those who watch.

The Lord may give to some upon occasion, a hint or encouragement out of the common way. But to seek His direction in such things as just mentioned is unscriptural and ensnaring. Some presumed they were doing God's service while acting in contradiction to His express commands. Others were infatuated to believe a lie, declaring themselves assured beyond the shadow of a doubt of things which never came to pass. When they were disappointed, Satan improved the occasion to make them doubt the plainest and most important truths, and to count their whole former experience as a delusion. These things have caused weak believers to stumble, offenses against the Gospel have multiplied, and evil spoken of the way of truth.

How, then, may the Lord's guidance be expected? After all these negative premises, the question may be answered in a few words. In general, He directs His people by affording them, in answer to prayer, the light of His Holy Spirit, which enables them to understand and love the Scriptures. The Word of God is not to be used as a lottery, nor is it designed to instruct us by shreds and scraps, which detached from their proper places have no determined import. But it is to furnish us with just principles, right apprehensions, to regulate our judgments and affections thereby to influence and regulate our conduct. Those who study the Scriptures in humble dependence upon divine teaching are convinced of their own weakness. They are taught to make a true estimate of everything around them and are gradually formed into a spirit of submission to the will of God. They discover the nature and duties of their situations and relations in life, and the snares and temptations to which they are exposed. The Word of God dwelling in them is a preservative from error, a light to their feet, and a spring of strength and consolation. By treasuring up the doctrines, precepts, promises, examples, and exhortations of Scripture in their minds—and daily comparing them with the rule by which they walk—they grow into an habitual frame of spiritual wisdom. They acquire a gracious taste which enables them to judge right and wrong with a degree of certainty, as a musical ear judges sounds. They are seldom mistaken, because they are influenced by the love of Christ which rules in their hearts, and a regard for the glory of God.

In particular cases, the Lord opens and shuts for them, breaks down walls of difficulty which obstruct their path, or hedges up their way with thorns when they are in danger of going wrong. They know their concerns are in His hands; they are willing to follow where and when He leads but are afraid of running before Him. They are not impatient. Because they believe, they will not be hasty, but wait daily upon Him in prayer, especially when they find their hearts engaged in any pursuit. They are jealous of being deceived by appearances, and dare not move farther or faster than they can see His light shining upon their paths. I express at least their desire, if not their attainment. Though there are seasons when faith languishes, and self prevails too much, this is their general disposition. And the Lord does not disappoint their expectations. He leads them on a right way, preserves them from a thousand snares, and satisfies them that He is and will be their Guide even unto death.

The positive side of the subject probably needs some amplification. The general rule may be stated thus: if we are daily concerned in seeking to please God in all the details, great and small, of our lives. He will not leave us in ignorance of His will concerning us. But if we are accustomed to gratify self and only turn up to God for help in times of difficulty and emergency, then we must not be surprised if He mocks us and allows us to reap the fruits of our folly. Our business is to walk in obedient subjection to Christ, and His sure promise is, "he who follows me shall not walk in darkness" (John 8:12). Make sure you sincerely endeavor to follow the example Christ left us, and He will not leave you in uncertainty as to which step you should take when you come to the place of decision.

"Therefore do not be unwise, but understand what the Lord's will is." (Eph. 5:17). From this verse it is clear that it is both the right and the duty of the Christian to know the Lord's will for him. God can neither be pleased nor glorified by His children walking in ignorance or proceeding blindly. Did not

Christ say to His beloved disciples, "Henceforth I call you not servants; for the servant knows not what His Lord does: but I have called you friends, for all things that I have heard from my Father I have made known unto you" (John 15:15). If we are in the dark as to how we ought to proceed in anything, it is clear that we are living far below our privileges. No doubt the majority of our readers will give hearty assent to these statements, but the question which concerns most of them is, How are we to ascertain the Lord's will concerning the varied details of our lives?

First, notice this exhortation, that we should be understanding "what the will of the Lord is," is preceded by "Therefore do not be foolish." That word "foolish" signifies no more than it now does in common speech. In Scripture the fool is not simply one who is mentally deficient, but is the man who leaves God out of his life, who acts independently of Him. This must be borne in mind as we arrive at the meaning of the second half of Ephesians 5:17.

Observe that Ephesians 5:17 opens with the word "Therefore," which points back to what immediately precedes: "See then that you walk circumspectly, not as fools, but as wise, redeeming the time, because the days are evil" (vv. 15-16). Unless those exhortations are prayerfully and diligently heeded, it is impossible that we "understand what the will of the Lord is." Unless our walk be right there can be no spiritual discernment of God's will for us. This brings us back to a central thought. Our daily walk is to be ordered by God's Word. In proportion as it is so, we will be kept in His will and preserved from folly and sin.

"A good understanding have all those who do His commandments" (Psalm 111:10). A good understanding may be defined as spiritual instinct. We all know what is meant by the instinct with which the Creator has endowed animals and birds. It is an inward faculty which prompts them to avoid danger and moves them to seek what is for their well-being. Man was endowed originally with a similar instinct, though of a far superior order to that of lower creatures. But at the fall, he, to a large extent, lost it. As one generation of depraved beings followed another, their instinct has become more and more weakened, until now we see many conducting themselves with far less intelligence than the beasts of the field. They rush madly to destruction, which the instinct of the brutes would avoid. They act foolishly, yes, madly, contrary even to common sense, in conducting their affairs and concerns without discretion.

At regeneration, God gives His elect "the spirit . . . of a sound mind" (2 Tim. 1:7), but that spirit has to be cultivated. It needs training and direction. The necessary instruction is found in the Word. From that Word we learn what things will prove beneficial to us, and what will be injurious; what things to seek after, and what to avoid. As the precepts of Scripture are reduced to practice by us, and as its prohibitions and warnings are heeded, we are able to judge things in their true light. We are delivered from being deceived by false appearances, we are kept from making foolish mistakes. The closer we walk by the Word, the more fully this will prove to be the case with us: a good judgment or spiritual instinct will form in us, so that we conduct our affairs discreetly and adorn the doctrine we profess.

So highly does the saint prize this spiritual instinct or sound mind, that he prays "Teach me good judgment and knowledge: for I have believed your commandments" (Psalm 119:66). He realizes it can only be increased as he is divinely taught by the Spirit applying the Word to his heart, opening to him its meaning, bringing it to his remembrance when needed, and enabling him to make a proper use of it. But note that in this prayer the petition is backed up with a plea, "for I have believed in Your commandments." "Believed" is not merely an intellectual assent, but approved with the affections. Only when that is the case is such a petition sincere. There is an inseparable connection between these two things. Where God's commandments are loved by us, we can count upon Him to teach us good judgment.

As we said, the "fool" is not the mentally deficient, but the one who leaves God out of his thoughts and plans, who cares not whether his conduct pleases or displeases Him. The fool is a godless person. Contrariwise, the "wise" (in Scripture) are not the highly intellectual or the brilliantly educated, but those who honestly seek to put God first in their lives. God "honors" those who honor Him (1 Sam. 2:30). He gives them "good judgment." True, it is not acquired all in a day, but "here a little and there a little." Yet the more completely we surrender to God, the more the principles of His Word regulate our conduct, the swifter will be our growth in spiritual wisdom. In saying that this good judgment is not acquired all at once, we do not mean that a whole lifetime has to be lived before it becomes ours, though this is often the case with many. Some who have been converted but a few years are often more spiritual, godly, and possess more spiritual wisdom than those who were converted years before.

By treasuring up in his mind the doctrines, precepts, promises, exhortations, and warnings of Scripture, and by diligently comparing himself with the rule by which he is to walk, the Christian grows into a habitual frame of spiritual wisdom. He acquires a gracious taste which enables him to judge of right and wrong with a degree of readiness and certainty, as a musical ear judges sounds, so that he is rarely mistaken. He who has the Word ruling in his heart is influenced by it in all his actions. Because the glory of God is the great aim before him, he is not permitted to go far wrong. Moreover, God has promised to show Himself strong on behalf of the one whose heart is perfect toward Him. He does this by regulating His providences and causing all things to work together for his good.

"The light of the body is the eye: if therefore your eye is single, your whole body shall be full of light" (Matthew 6:22). The language is figurative, yet its meaning is not difficult to ascertain. What the eye is to the body, the heart is to the soul, for out of the heart are "the issues of life" (Proverbs 4:23). The actions of the body are directed by the light received from the eye. If the eye is single, that is, sound and clear, perceiving objects as they really are—then the whole body has light to direct its members, and the man moves with safety and comfort. In like manner, if the heart is undivided, set on pleasing God in all things, then the soul has clear vision, discerning the true nature of things, forming a sound judgment of their worth, choosing wisely, and directing itself prudently. When the heart is right with God, the soul is endowed with spiritual wisdom, so that there is full light for our path.

"But if your eye is evil, your whole body shall be full of darkness. If therefore the light that is in you is darkness, how great is that darkness"! (Matthew 6:23). Here is the solemn contrast. If the vision of our bodily eye is defective, a cataract dimming it, then nothing is seen clearly. All is confusion, the man stumbles as if in the dark, as if continually liable to lose his way and run into danger. In like manner, where the heart is not right with God, where sin and self dominate, the whole soul is under the reign of darkness. In consequence, the judgment is blinded so that it cannot rightly discern between good and evil, cannot see through the gild of Satan's baits, and thus is fatally deceived by them. The very light which is in fallen man, namely his reason, is controlled by his lusts—so great is his darkness.

The verses we have just considered were spoken by Christ immediately after what He had been saying about the right laying up of treasures (Matthew 6:19-21). It was as though He both anticipated and answered a question from His disciples. If it is so important for us not to lay up treasures in earth, but rather treasures in heaven, why is it that the men commonly regarded as the shrewdest, and considered to be the most successful, seek after earthly treasures, rather than heavenly? To this Christ replied: marvel not at this—they cannot see what they are doing: they are like blind men gathering pebbles—and supposing that they are valuable diamonds.

Christ casts much light on what we now see on every side. Those who have set their hearts on things of time and sense, are but spending their energies for that which will stand them in no stead when they come to their deathbeds. They labor for that which satisfies not (Isaiah 55:2). The reason they conduct themselves so insanely—pursuing so eagerly the pleasures of this world, which will bear nothing but bitter regrets in the world to come—is because their hearts are evil. God has no real place in their thoughts, and so He gives them up to the spirit of madness. There must be the single eye—the heart set upon pleasing God—if the soul is to be filled with heavenly wisdom, which loves, seeks, and lays up heavenly things. That wisdom is something which no university can impart. It is "from above" (Jam. 3:17).

It should be noted that our Lord's teaching upon the "single eye," with the whole body "full of light," and the "evil eye" with the whole body "full of darkness," is immediately followed with, "No man can serve two masters: for either he will hate the one, and love the other; or else he will hold to the one, and despise the other. You cannot serve God and mammon" (Matthew 6:24). This at once establishes the meaning of the preceding verses. Christ had been speaking (in a figure) of setting the Lord supremely before the heart, which necessarily involves casting out worldly things and fleshly considerations. Men think to have both God and their lusts, both God and mammon, both God and worldly pleasures. No! says Christ. God will have all or nothing. He who serves Him must serve Him singly and supremely. Are you willing to pay the price to have divine light on your path?

We have not attempted to enter into specific details and state how a person is to act when some difficult or sudden emergency confronts him. Rather we have sought to treat of basic principles and thoroughly establish them. Though it might satisfy curiosity, it would serve no good purpose for a teacher to explain an intricate problem in higher mathematics to a student who had not already mastered the elementary rules of arithmetic. So it would be out of place to explain how particular cases or circumstances are to be handled before we have presented those rules which must guide our general walk.

Thus far we have dealt with two main things: the absolute necessity of being controlled by the Word of God in our outward walk; and the having a heart within which is single to God's glory and set upon pleasing Him—if we are to have the light of heaven on our earthly path.

A third consideration must now engage our attention: the help of the Holy Spirit. But at this point we most need to be on our guard, lest we lapse into a vague mysticism on the one hand, or become guilty of wild fanaticism on the other. Many have plunged into the most foolish and evil courses under the plea they were "prompted by the Spirit." No doubt they were prompted by some spirit, but most certainly not by the Holy Spirit. HE never prompts anything contrary to the Word. Our only safety is to impartially bring our inward impulses to the test of Holy Writ.

"For as many as are led by the Spirit of God, they are the sons of God" (Romans 8:14). This divine Guide is perfectly acquainted with the path God has ordained for each celestial traveler. He is fully conversant with all its windings and narrowness, its intricacies and dangers. To be led by the Spirit is to be under His government. He perceives our temptations and weakness, knows our aspirations, hears our groans, and marks our strugglings after holiness. He knows when to supply a check, administer a rebuke, apply a promise, sympathize with a sorrow, strengthen a wavering purpose, confirm a fluctuating hope. The sure promise is, "He will guide you into all truth" (John 16:13). He does so by regulating our thoughts, affections and conduct; by opening our understandings to perceive the meaning of Scripture, applying it in power to the heart, enabling us to appropriate and reduce it to practice. Each time we open the sacred volume, let us humbly and earnestly seek the aid of Him who inspired it.

Note that Romans 8:14 opens with "for." The apostle introduces a confirmation of what he had affirmed in the previous verses. Those who "walk not after the flesh, but after the Spirit" (verse 4); those who mind "the things of the Spirit" (verse 5); those who "through the Spirit do mortify the deeds of the body" (verse 13)—are the ones who are "led by the Spirit." As the Spirit of holiness, His aim is to deepen the imprint of the restored image of God in the soul, to increase our happiness by making us more holy. Thus He leads to nothing but what is sanctifying. The Spirit guides by subduing the power of indwelling sin, by weaning us from the world, by maintaining a tender conscience in us, by drawing out the heart to Christ, by causing us to live for eternity.

"Trust in the Lord with all your heart; and do not lean on your own understanding: in all your ways acknowledge Him, and He shall direct your paths" (Proverbs 3:5-6). Note the order: the promise at the close of the passage is conditional upon our meeting three requirements.

First, we are to have full confidence in the Lord. The Hebrew verb for "trust" here literally means "to lean upon." It conveys the idea of one who is conscious of feebleness turning unto and resting upon a stronger one for support. To "trust in the Lord" signifies to count upon Him in every emergency, to look to Him for the supply of every need, to say with the psalmist, "The Lord is my shepherd; I shall not lack" (Psalm 23:1). It means that we cast all our cares upon Him, draw from Him strength hour by hour and thus prove the sufficiency of His grace. It means for the Christian to continue as he began. When we first cast ourselves upon Him as lost sinners, we abandoned all our own doings and relied upon His abounding mercy.

But what is meant by "trust in the Lord with all your heart?"
First, the giving to God our undivided confidence, not looking to any other for help and relief.

Second, turning to Him with childlike simplicity. When a little one trusts, there is no reasoning, but a simple taking of the parent's words at face value, fully assured that he will make good what he said; he does not dwell on the difficulties in the way, but expects a fulfillment of what is promised. So it should be with us and our heavenly Father's words.

Third, it means with our affections going out to Him, "love believes all things, hopes all things," (1 Cor. 13:7). Thus, to trust in the Lord "with all our heart" is love's reliance in believing dependence and expectation.

The second requirement is, "and do not lean on your own understanding," which means we are not to trust in our own wisdom or rely upon the dictates of human reason. The highest act of human reason is to disown its sufficiency and bow before the wisdom of God. To lean on our own understanding is to rest upon a broken reed, for it has been deranged by sin. Yet many find it harder to repudiate their own wisdom than they do to abandon their own righteousness. Many of God's ways are "past finding out." To seek to solve the mysteries of Providence is the finite attempting to comprehend the Infinite. Philosophizing about our lot, or reasoning about our circumstances, is fatal to rest of soul and peace of heart.

Third, "in all your ways acknowledge Him." This means, first, we must ask God's permission for all that we do, and not act without His permission.

Only then do we conduct ourselves as dutiful children and respectful servants. It means, second, that we seek God's guidance in every undertaking, acknowledging our ignorance and owning our complete dependence upon Him. "In everything by prayer and supplication" (Phil. 4:6). Only so is God's lordship over us owned in a practical way. It means, third, seeking God's glory in all our ways, "Whatever you do—do all to the glory of God" (1 Cor. 10:31). If we only did so, how very different many of our ways would be! If more frequently we paused and inquired—Will this be for God's glory? we would be withheld from much sinning and folly, with all its painful consequences. It means, fourth, to seek God's blessing upon everything. Here is another simple and sufficient rule: anything on which I cannot ask God's blessing is wrong.

"And He shall direct your paths." Meet the three conditions just mentioned and this is the sure consequence. The need to be directed by God is real and pressing. Left to ourselves we are no better off than a rudderless ship, or an automobile without a steering wheel. It is not without reason that the Lord's people are so often termed "sheep," for no other creature is so apt to stray or has such a propensity to wander. The Hebrew word for "direct" means "to make straight." We live in a world where everything is crooked. Sin has thrown everything out of joint, and in consequence confusion abounds all around us. A deceitful heart, a wicked world, and a subtle devil—ever seek to lead us astray and compass our destruction. How necessary it is, then, for God to "direct my paths."

What is meant by "He shall direct your paths?" It means, He will make clear to me the course of duty. God's "will" always lies in the path of duty, and never runs counter to it. Much needless uncertainty would be spared if only this principle were recognized. When you feel a strong desire or prompting to shirk a plain duty, you may be assured it is a temptation from Satan, and not the leading of the Holy Spirit. For example, it is contrary to God's revealed will for a woman to be constantly attending meetings to the neglect of her children and home. It is shirking his responsibility for a husband to get off alone in the evenings, even in religious exercises, and leave his tired wife to wash the dishes and put the children to bed. It is a sin for a Christian employee to read the Scriptures or "speak to people about their souls" during business hours.

The difficulty arises when it appears we have to choose between two or more duties, or when some important change has to be made in our circumstances. There are many people who think they need to be guided by God when some crisis arrives or some important decision has to be made. But few of them are prepared to meet the requirements intimated in the Scriptures. The fact is, that God was rarely in their thoughts before the emergency arose. Pleasing Him did not exercise them while things were going smoothly. But when difficulty confronts them, when they are at their wits end on how to act, they suddenly become very pious, turn to the Lord, earnestly ask Him to direct them and make His way plain.

But God cannot be imposed upon in any such manner. Usually such people make a rash decision and bring themselves into still greater difficulties. Then they attempt to console themselves with, "Well, I sought God's guidance." God is not to be mocked like that. If we ignore His claims on us when the sailing is pleasant, we cannot count upon Him to deliver us when the storm comes. The One we have to do with is holy, and He will not set a premium upon godlessness (called by many "carelessness"), even though we howl like beasts when in anguish (Hos. 7:14). On the other hand, if we diligently seek grace to walk with God day by day, regulating our ways by His commandments, then we may rightfully count upon His aid in every emergency that arises.

But how is the conscientious Christian to act when some emergency confronts him? Suppose he stands at the dividing of the ways. Two paths, two alternatives, are before him, and he does not know which to choose. What must he do? First, let him heed that most necessary word, which as a rule of general application is ever binding upon us, "he who believes shall not make haste" (Isaiah 28:16). To act from a sudden impulse never befits a child of God, and to rush ahead of the Lord is sure to involve us in painful consequences. "The Lord is good unto those who wait for him, to the soul who seeks him. It is good that a man should both hope, and quietly wait for the salvation [deliverance] of the Lord" (Lam. 3:25-26). To act in haste generally means that afterward we repent at leisure. How much each of us needs to beg the Lord to daily lay His quietening hand upon our feverish flesh!

Second, ask the Lord for Him to empty your heart of every wish of your own. It is impossible for us to sincerely pray, "Your will be done"—until our own will has, by the power of the Holy Spirit, been brought into complete subjection to God. Just so long as there is a secret (but real) preference in my heart, my judgment will be biased. While my heart is really set upon the attainment of a certain object, then I only mock God when I ask Him to make His way plain; and I am sure to misinterpret all His providences, twisting them to fit my own desire. If an obstacle is in my path, I then regard it as a "testing of faith"; if a barrier is removed, I at once jump to the conclusion that God is undertaking for me, when instead He may be testing me, on the eve of giving me up to my own "heart's lust" (Psalm 81:12).

This point is of supreme importance for those who desire their steps to be truly ordered of the Lord. We cannot discern His best for us while the heart has its own preference. Thus it is imperative to ask God to empty our hearts of all personal preferences, to remove any secret, set desire of our own. But often it is not easy to take this attitude before God, the more so if we are not in the habit of seeking grace to mortify the flesh. By nature each of us wants his own way, and chafes against every curb placed upon us. Just as a photographic plate must be blank if it is to receive a picture upon it, so our hearts must be free from personal bias if God is to work in us "both to will and to do of his good pleasure" (Phil. 2:13).

If you find that as you continue to wait upon God, the inward struggle between the flesh and the spirit continues, and you have not reached the point where you can honestly say, "Have Your own way, Lord," then a season of fasting is in order. Ezra 8:21 reads, "Then I proclaimed a fast there . . . that we might afflict ourselves before our God, to seek of him a right way for us, and for our little ones." This is written for our instruction, and even a glance at it shows it is pertinent. Nor is fasting a religious exercise peculiar to Old Testament times. Acts 13:3 records that before Barnabas and Saul were sent forth on their missionary journey by the church at Antioch, "When they had fasted and prayed, and laid their hands on them, they sent them away." There is nothing meritorious in fasting—but it expresses humility of soul and earnestness of heart.

The next thing is to humbly and sincerely acknowledge to God our ignorance—and request Him not to leave us to ourselves. Tell Him frankly you are perplexed and do not know what to do. But plead before Him His own promise, and ask Him for Christ's sake to make it good to you. "If any of you lacks wisdom, he should ask God, who gives generously to all without finding fault, and it will be given to him. But when he asks, he must believe and not doubt, because he who doubts is like a wave of the sea, blown and tossed by the wind." (James 1:5-6). Ask Him to grant the wisdom you need so much, that you may judge rightly, that you may discern clearly what will promote your spiritual welfare, and therefore be most for His glory.

"Commit your way unto the Lord, trust also in him; and he shall bring it to pass" (Psalm 37:5). In the interval if you go to fellow-Christians for advice, most probably no two will agree, and their discordant counsel will only confuse. Instead of looking to man for help, "Continue in prayer, and watch in the same with thanksgiving" (Col. 4:2). Be on the lookout for God's answer. Mark attentively each movement of His providence, for as a straw in the air indicates which way the wind is blowing so the hand of God may often be discerned by a spiritual eye in what are trifling incidents to others. "And let it be, when you hear the sound of a going in the tops of the mulberry trees, that then you shall bestir yourself: for then shall the Lord go out before you" (2 Sam. 5:24).

Finally, remember that we need not only light from the Lord to discover our duty in particular cases, but when that has been obtained, we need His presence to accompany us, so that we may be enabled to rightly follow the path He bids us go. Moses realized this when he said to the Lord, "If your presence goes not with me, carry us not up hence" (Ex. 33:15). If we do not have the presence of God with us in an undertaking—His approval upon it, His assistance in it, His blessing upon it—then we find it a snare—if not a curse to us.

As a general rule it is better for us to trouble our minds very little about guidance. That is God's work. Our business is to walk in obedience to Him day by day. As we do so, there works within us a prudence which will preserve us from all serious mistakes. "I understand more than the ancients, because I keep your precepts" (Psalm 119:100). The man who keeps God's precepts is endowed with a wisdom which far surpasses that possessed by the sages or the learned philosophers. "Unto the upright there arises light in the darkness" (Psalm 112:4). The upright man may experience his days of darkness, but when the hour of emergency arrives, light will be given him by God. Serve God with all your might today—and you may calmly and safely leave the future with Him. A duteous conformity to what is right—will be followed by luminous discernment of what would be wrong.

Seek earnestly to get the fear of God fixed in your heart so that you tremble at His Word (Isaiah 66:2) and are really afraid to displease Him. "Who, then, is the man that fears the Lord? He will instruct him in the way chosen for him" (Psalm 25:12). "Behold, the fear of the Lord, that is wisdom;

and to depart from evil is understanding" (Job 28:28). "Then shall we know, if we follow on to know the Lord" (Hos. 6:3). The more we grow in grace—the fuller our knowledge will be of God's revealed will. The more we cultivate the practice of seeking to please God in all things—the more light we will have for our path. "The pure in heart shall see God" (Matthew 5:8). If our motive is right—our vision will be clear.

"The integrity of the upright guides them, but the perversity of the treacherous destroys them" (Proverbs 11:3). The upright man will not willingly and knowingly go aside into crooked paths. The honest heart is not bewildered by domineering lusts nor blinded by corrupt motives. Having a tender conscience he possesses keen spiritual discernment; but the crooked policy of the wicked involves them in increasing trouble and ends in their eternal ruin. "The righteousness of the blameless makes a straight way for them, but the wicked are brought down by their own wickedness." (Proverbs 11:5). An eye single to God's glory delivers from those snares in which the ungodly are taken. Unbridled passions becloud the understanding and pervert the judgment, until men call good "evil" and evil "good" (Isaiah 5:20); but he who seeks to be subject to the Lord, shall be given discretion.

"The Lord shall direct your paths." First, by His Word: not in some magical way so as to encourage laziness, nor like consulting a cookbook full of recipes for all occasions—but by warning us of the byways of sin and making known the paths of righteousness and blessing. Second, by his Spirit: giving us strength to obey the precepts of God, causing us to wait patiently on the Lord for directions, enabling us to apply the rules of Holy Writ to the varied duties of our lives, bringing to our remembrance a word in due season. Third, by His providences: causing friends to fail us so that we are delivered from leaning upon the arm of flesh, thwarting our carnal plans so that we are preserved from shipwreck, shutting doors which it would not be good for us to enter—and opening doors before us which none can shut.

CHAPTER 22
The Blessings of God

"The blessing of the Lord brings wealth, and He adds no trouble to it" (Proverbs 10:22). Temporal blessing, as well as spiritual, comes from Him. "The Lord makes poor, and makes rich" (1 Sam. 2:7). God is the sovereign disposer of material wealth. If it is received by birth or inheritance—it is by His providence. If it comes by gift—He moved the donors to bestow. If it accumulates as the result of hard work, skill, or thrift—He bestowed the talent, directed its use, and granted the success. This is abundantly clear in the Scriptures. "The Lord has blessed my master greatly . . . he has given him flocks, and herds, and silver, and gold" (Gen. 24:35). "Isaac planted crops in that land and the same year reaped a hundredfold, because the Lord blessed him" (Gen. 26:12). So it is with us. Then say not in your heart, "The might of my hand or brains has gotten me this temporal prosperity." "But you shall remember the Lord your God: for it is he who gives you power to get wealth" (Deut. 8:18). When riches are acquired by God's blessing by honest industry, there is no accusing conscience to sour the same. If sorrow attends the use or enjoyment of them, it is due entirely to our own folly.

"Blessed is the man whom you chose, and cause to approach unto you, that he may dwell in your courts" (Psalm 65:4). There is no doubt that the primary reference there (though not the exclusive one) is to "the man Christ Jesus" (1 Tim. 2:5), for as God-man He is what He is by the grace of election, when His humanity was chosen and foreordained to union with one of the Persons in the Godhead. None other than Jehovah proclaimed Him, "my elect, in whom my soul delighted" (Isaiah 42:1). As such He is, "The man who is my fellow, says the Lord Almighty" (Zech. 13:7), the "heir of all things." Christ was not chosen for us, but for God; and we were chosen for Christ, to be His bride. "Christ is My first elect He said, then chose our souls in Christ the Head." The essence of all blessings is to be in Christ, and those who partake of it do so by the act of God, as the fruit of His everlasting love unto them.

"Blessed be the God and Father of our Lord Jesus Christ, who has blessed us with every spiritual blessing in the heavens, in Christ; for He chose us in Him, before the foundation of the world, to be holy and blameless in His sight." (Eph. 1:3-4). In that initial blessing of election all others are wrapped up, and in due course we are partakers of them. It is both the duty and privilege of every sin-laden soul to come to Christ for rest; nevertheless it is equally true that no man can come to Him unless the Father draws him (John 6:44). Likewise it falls upon all who hear the Gospel to respond to that call. "Incline your ear, and come unto me: hear, and your soul shall live" (Isaiah 55:3), yet how can those who are dead in trespasses and sins (Eph. 2:1) do so? They cannot. They must first be divinely quickened into newness of life.

A beautiful figure of that divine operation is here before us. In eastern lands the earth is hard, dry, barren. So are our natural hearts. The dew descends from above silently, mysteriously, imperceptibly and moistens the ground, imparting vitality to vegetation, making the mountainside fruitful. Such is the miracle of the new birth. Life is communicated by divine fiat; not a probationary or conditional one, not a fleeting or temporal one, but spiritual and endless, for the stream of regeneration can never dry up. When God commands, He communicates (cf. Psalm 42:8; 48:28; 111:9). As the blessing is a divine favor, so the manner of bestowing it is sovereign. That is solely His prerogative, for man can do nothing but beg. Zion is the place of all spiritual blessings (Heb. 12:22-24).

"Blessed is the people who know the joyful sound: they shall walk, O Lord, in the light of Your countenance" (Psalm 89:15). This is one of the blessed effects of Divine quickening. When one has been born of the Spirit, the eyes and ears of his soul are opened to recognize spiritual things. It is not merely that they "hear the joyful sound," for many do that without any experiential knowledge of its charm; but know from its message being brought home in power to their hearts. That joyful sound is the "glad tidings of good things" (Romans 10:15), namely, "that Christ Jesus came into the world to save sinners." Such souls as inwardly know that heavenly music are indeed blessed. As they are assured of free access unto God through the blood of Christ, the beneficent light of the divine countenance is now beheld by them. There is probably an allusion in Psalm 89:15, First to the sound made by Aaron as he went into the holy place and came out (Ex. 28:33-35), which was indeed a "joyful sound" unto the people of God. It gave evidence that their high priest was engaged before the Lord on their behalf. Second, a general reference to the sound of the sacred trumpets which called Israel to their solemn feasts (Num. 10:10). Third, a more specific one to the trumpet of jubilee (Lev. 25:9-10), which proclaimed liberty to bondmen and restoration of their inheritance to them who had forfeited it. So the announcement of the Gospel of liberty to sin's captives is music to those who have ears to hear.

"Blessed are all those who put their trust in him" (Psalm 2:12). The critical reader observes that we follow a strictly logical order. First, election is the foundation blessing, being "unto salvation" and including all the means thereof (2 Thess. 2:13); second, the bestowal of eternal life which capacitates the favored recipient to welcome experientially the joyful sound of the Gospel. Now there is a personal and saving embracing thereof. Note that the words of our present text are preceded by "Kiss the Son," which signifies, "Bow in submission before His scepter, yield to His Kingly rule, render allegiance to Him" (1 Sam. 10:1; 1 Kings 19:18). It is most important to note that order, and still more so to put it into practice. Christ must be received as Lord (Col. 2:6) before He can be received as Savior. Note the order in 2 Peter 1:11; 2:20; 3:18. The "put their trust in Him" signifies to take refuge in. They repudiate their own righteousness and evince their confidence in Him by committing themselves to His keeping for time and eternity. His Gospel is their warrant for doing so, His veracity their security.

"Blessed is he whose transgression is forgiven, whose sin is covered" (Psalm 32:1). This is an intrinsic part of the blessedness of putting our trust in Him. The joyful sound has assured them that "Christ died for the ungodly," and that He will by no means cast out anyone who comes unto Him. Therefore do they express their faith in Christ by fleeing to Him for refuge. Blessed indeed are such, for, having surrendered to His lordship and placed their reliance in His atoning blood, they now enter into the benefits of His righteous and benevolent government. More specifically, their "iniquities are forgiven and their sins are covered"—"covered by God, as the ark was covered with the mercy-seat; as Noah was covered from the flood; as the Egyptians were covered by the depths of the sea. What a cover that must be which hides forever from the sight of the all-seeing God all the filthiness of the flesh and of the spirit" (Charles Spurgeon). Paul quotes those precious words of Psalm 32:1 in Romans 4:7, as proof of the grand truth of justification by faith. While the sins of believers were all atoned for at the cross and an everlasting righteousness procured for them, they do not become actual participants until they believe (Acts 13:39; Gal. 2:16).

"Blessed are those whose strength is in you, who have set their hearts on pilgrimage" (Psalm 84:5). This is another accompaniment of the new birth. The regenerated receives the spirit of "a sound mind" (2 Tim. 1:7) so that he now sees himself to be not only without any righteousness of his own, but also is conscious of his weakness and insufficiency. He has made the name of the Lord his strong tower, having run into it for safety (Proverbs 18:10). Now he declares, "in the Lord I have righteousness and strength" (Isaiah 45:24), strength to fight the good fight of faith, to resist temptations, to endure persecution, to perform duty. While he keeps in his right mind, he will continue to go forth not in his own strength, but in complete dependence upon the strength in Christ Jesus. Those ways of God's strength are the divinely appointed means of grace to maintain communion: feeding on the Word, living on Christ, adhering to the path of His precepts.

"Blessed is everyone who fears the Lord; who walks in his ways" (Psalm 128:1). Here is another mark of those under divine benediction: to have such a deep reverence of the Spirit as results in regular obedience to Him. The fear of the Lord is a holy awe of His majesty, a filial dread of displeasing Him. It is not so much an emotional thing as practical, for it is idle to talk about fearing God if we have no deep concern for His will. It is the fear of love which shrinks from dishonoring Him, a dread of forgetting His goodness and abusing His mercy. Where such fear is, all other graces are found.

CHAPTER 23
The Cursings of God

It is solemn to learn that these blessings and cursings proceed from the same mouth. Yet a little reflection will convince the reader that such must be the case. God is light as well as love, holy as well as gracious, righteous as well as merciful. Therefore He expresses His abhorrence of and visits His judgments upon the wicked, as truly as He blesses and manifests His approval on those who are pleasing in His sight. An eternal heaven and an eternal hell are the inevitable and ultimate pair of opposites. This awesome duality is displayed in the natural world. On one hand our senses are charmed by the golden sunsets, the flowering gardens, the gentle showers and the fertile fields. On the other hand, we are shocked and terrified by the fearful tornado, the devouring blights, the devastating flood, and the destructive earthquake. "Behold therefore the goodness and severity of God" (Romans 11:22). From Mt. Ebal were announced the divine curses (Deut. 27), and from Matthew Gerizim the divine blessings (Deut. 28). The one could not be without the other. Thus too it will be in the last day, or while Christ will say unto His brethren, "Come you blessed of my Father, inherit the kingdom prepared for you from the foundation of the world," yet to those who despised and rejected Him shall He say "Depart from me, you cursed, into everlasting fire'" (Matthew 25:34, 41).

"Cursed is the ground for your sake; in sorrow shall you eat of it all the days of your life" (Gen. 3:17). That was one of the consequences which attended Adam's apostasy from God, a part of the divine vengeance which fell upon him. Because the first man stood as the covenant head and legal representative of his race, the judgment which came upon him is shared by all his descendants. Adam was the vice-regent of God in this scene. He was given dominion over all things mundane, and when he fell, the effects of his awful sin were evident on every hand. His fair inheritance was blasted. The very ground on which he trod was cursed, so that henceforth it brought forth "thorns and thistles," compelling him to toil for his daily bread in the sweat of his face. Every time we cultivate a plot of land, the numerous weeds it produces hinder our efforts and supply very real proof of the divine sentence pronounced in Genesis 3 and evince that we belong to a fallen race.

"Thus says the Lord; Cursed is the one who trusts in man, who depends on flesh for his strength and whose heart turns away from the Lord" (Jer. 17:5). A thorough acquaintance with ourselves ought to render the warning of this solemn passage unnecessary, yet sad experience proves otherwise. Have we not sufficient knowledge of ourselves—our changeableness and utter unreliability—to discover that "he who trusts in his own heart is a fool" (Proverbs 28:26)? Then why should we suppose that any of our fellows are more stable and dependable? The best of Adam's race, when left to themselves, are spectacles of fickleness and frailty. "Lowborn men are but a breath, the highborn are but a lie; if weighed on a balance, they are nothing; together they are only a breath" (Psalm 62:9). To seek either the patronage or protection of man is an affront to the Most High, for it puts that confidence in the creature to which the Creator alone is entitled. The folly of such wickedness is emphasized in," leaning upon that which is frail and helpless (2 Chron. 32:8; Matthew 26:41; Romans 8:3). The Christian needs to turn this awful malediction into prayer for deliverance from the temptation to look to man for help or relief! Indirectly, yet powerfully, this verse proves that Christ is far more than man; for if it calls down a divine curse for one to put his trust in man for any temporal advantage, how much more so if he trusts in a mere creature for eternal salvation!

"If you do not listen, and if you do not set your heart to honor my name," says the Lord Almighty, "I will send a curse upon you, and I will curse your blessings. Yes, I have already cursed them, because you have not set your heart to honor me" (Mal. 2:2). The Lord is very tender of His honor and will not share His glory with another (Isaiah 48:11), and those who do not take that fact to heart are certain to call down divine wrath upon themselves. Those words (Mal. 2:2) were addressed in the first instance to the priests of Israel. The prophet had reproved them for their sins. Now he declared that if they would not seriously attend to his warnings, and glorify God by repentance and reformation of conduct, then He would blight their temporal mercies. It is a signal favor for man to be called to minister publicly in the name of the Lord. But infidelity entails the most dreadful consequences. Often they are given up to blindness of mind, hardness of heart, seared consciences. The principle of this malediction has a much wider bearing and applies both to those who hear the Gospel, and a nation blessed with its light.

"But though we, or an angel from heaven, preach any other gospel unto you than that which we have preached unto you, let him be accursed" (Gal. 1:8). God is very jealous of His Gospel, and this verse should also convince His servants and people of the solemn responsibility resting upon them to preserve it in its purity. The Gospel of God makes known the only true way of salvation, and therefore any corrupting of it is not only dishonoring to its Author, but also most dangerous and disastrous to the souls of men. The apostle was censuring those who were repeating an impossible mixture of Law and Gospel, insisting that circumcision and compliance with the ceremonial rites of Judaism were as necessary as faith in Christ for justification. His was not the language of intemperate zeal, for he repeats the same in the next verse, but a holy fidelity, which expressed his detestation of an error which not only insulted the Savior but also would prove fatal to those who embraced it. The single foundation of a sinner's hope is the merits of Christ, His finished work of redemption. Those who would add to the same by any doings of their own are headed for eternal destruction. Therefore any who teach men to do so are cursed of God and should be abhorred by His people.

"For as many as are of the works of the law are under the curse: for it is written, Cursed is everyone who continues not in all things which are written in the book of the law to do them" (Gal. 3:10). The first part of this verse means: all who count on being saved by their own performances, or rely upon their own obedience for acceptance by God, are under the curse of His Law and exposed to His wrath. Justification by keeping the Law is an utter impossibility for any fallen creature. Why so? Because God's Law requires flawless and perpetual conformity, sinless perfection in thought and word and deed, and because it makes no provision for failure to comply with its holy and righteous terms. It is not sufficient to hear about or know the requirements of God's Law. They must be met. Thus it is obvious that a Law which already condemns, cannot justify; that any who hope to merit God's favor by their faulty attempts to obey it are badly deceived. "To expect to be warmed by the keen northern blast, or to have our thirst quenched by a draught of liquid fire, were not more, were not so, incongruous" (J. Brown). This statement (Gal. 3:10) was made by the apostle to show that every man is under divine condemnation until he flees to Christ for refuge.

"Christ has redeemed us from the curse of the law, being made a curse for us" (Gal. 3:13). Here is the glorious Gospel summed up in a brief sentence.

The curse has been borne for all those who believe—visited upon the Savior. A way has been opened where guilty sinners may not only escape from the curse of the Law, but actually be received into the favor of God. Amazing grace! Matchless mercy! All who put their trust in Christ are delivered from the Law's sentence of doom so that they shall never fall under it. We are righteously delivered, because as the Surety of His people Christ was born under the Law, stood in their law place, had all their sins imputed to Him, and made Himself answerable for them. The Law, so finding Him, charged Him with the same, cursed Him, and demanded satisfaction. Accordingly He was dealt with by the supreme Judge, for "God spared not His own Son," but called upon the sword of justice to smite the shepherd (Zech. 13:7). By His own consent the Lord Jesus was "made a curse" by God Himself. Because He paid the ransom price all believers are "redeemed"—delivered from God's wrath and inducted into His blessing.

"But that which bears thorns and briers is rejected, and is near unto cursing; whose end is to be burned" (Heb. 6:8). This is in sharp contrast with the previous verse. The good-ground hearer "brings forth"—the Greek signifying a production of what is normal and in due season. The graceless professor "bears thorns"—the Greek word connoting an unnatural and monstrous production. There, "herbs fit for them by whom it is dressed"; here, worthless "thorns and briers." The one "receives blessing from God", the other is "near unto cursing"—about to be visited with divine judgment.

CHAPTER 24
The Gospel of the Grace of God

"To testify the gospel of the grace of God" (Acts 20:24) formed part of the farewell address of the apostle Paul to the leaders of the church at Ephesus. After he reminded them of his manner of life among them (vv. 18-21), he tells them of his forthcoming trip to Jerusalem, which was to culminate in his being carried prisoner to Rome. He says, "And now, behold, I go bound in the spirit unto Jerusalem, not knowing the things that shall befall me there: save that the Holy Spirit witnesses in every city, saying that bonds and afflictions await me" (vv. 22-23). And, then, in a truly characteristic word he says, "But none of these things move me, neither count I my life dear unto myself, so that I might finish my course with joy, and the ministry, which I have received of the Lord Jesus, to testify the gospel of the grace of God" (v. 24). Wherever the providence of God might take him, whatever his circumstances might be, whether in bonds or in freedom, this should be his mission and message. It is to this same ministry that the Lord of the harvest still appoints His servants: to "testify the Gospel of the grace of God."

There is a continual need to return to the great fundamental of the faith. As long as the age lasts the Gospel of God's grace must be preached. The need arises out of the natural state of the human heart, which is essentially legalistic. The cardinal error against which the Gospel has to contend is the inveterate tendency of men to rely on their own performances. The great antagonist to the truth is the pride of man, which causes him to imagine that he can be, in part at least, his own savior. This error is the prolific mother of a multitude of heresies. It is by this falsehood that the pure stream of God's truth, passing through human channels, has been polluted.

Now the Gospel of God's grace is epitomized in Ephesians 2:8-9, "For by grace are you saved through faith; and that not of yourselves: it is the gift of God: not of works, lest any man should boast." All genuine reforms or revivals in the churches of God must have as their basis a plain declaration of this doctrine. The tendency of Christians is like that of the world, to shy away from this truth which is the very sum and substance of the Gospel.

Those with any acquaintance with Church history know how sadly true this is. Within fifty years of the death of the last of the apostles, so far as we can now learn, the Gospel of God's grace almost ceased to be preached. Instead of evangelizing, the preachers of the second and third centuries gave themselves to philosophizing. Philosophy took the place of the simplicity of the Gospel.

Then, in the fourth century, God mercifully raised up a man, Augustine, who faithfully and fearlessly proclaimed the Gospel. So mightily did God empower both his voice and pen that more than half of Christendom was shaken by him. Through his instrumentality came an heaven-sent revival. His influence for good staved off the great Romish heresy for another century. Had the churches heeded his teaching, popery would never have been born. But, they turned back to vain philosophy and science, falsely so-called.

Then came the Dark Ages, when for centuries the Gospel ceased to be generally preached. Here and there feeble voices were raised, but most of them were soon silenced by the Italian priests. It was not until the fifteenth century that the great Reformation came. God raised up Martin Luther, who taught in no uncertain terms that sinners are justified by faith, and not by works.

After Luther came a still more distinguished teacher, John Calvin. He was much more deeply taught in the truth of the Gospel, and pushed its central doctrine of grace to its logical conclusions. As Charles Spurgeon said, "Luther had, as it were, undammed the stream of truth, by breaking down the barriers which had kept back its living waters as in a great reservoir. But the stream was turbid and carried down with it much which ought to have been left behind. Then Calvin came, and cast salt into the waters, and purged them, so that there flowed on a purer stream to gladden and refresh souls and quench the thirst of poor lost sinners."

The great center of all Calvin's preaching was the grace of God. It has been the custom ever since to designate as "Calvinists" those who emphasize what he emphasized. We do not accept that title without qualification, but we certainly are not ashamed of it. The truth Calvin thundered forth was identical with the truth Paul had preached and set down in writing centuries before. This was also the substance of Whitefield's preaching, which God honored so extensively as to produce the great revival in his day. Let as now consider: The Gospel is a Revelation of the Grace of God.

The "Gospel of the grace of God" is one of the Holy Spirit's appellations of that Good News which the ambassadors of Christ are called upon to preach. Various names are given to it in the Scriptures. Romans 1:1 calls it the "gospel of God," for He is its Author. Romans 1:16 terms it the "gospel of Christ," for He is its theme. Ephesians 6:15 designates it the "gospel of peace," for this is its bestowment. Our text speaks of it as the "Gospel of the Grace of God," for this is its source.

Grace is a truth peculiar to divine revelation. It is a concept to which the unaided powers of man's mind never rises. Proof of this is in the fact that where the Bible has not gone "grace" is unknown. Very often missionaries have found, when translating the Scriptures into native tongues of the heathen, they were unable to discover a word which in any way corresponds to the Bible word "grace." Grace is absent from all the great heathen religions—Brahmanism, Buddhism, Mohammedanism, Confucianism, Zoroastrianism. Even nature does not teach grace: break her laws and you must suffer the penalty.

What then is grace?

First, it is evidently something very blessed and joyous, for our text speaks of the "good news of the grace of God."

Secondly, it is the opposite of Law: Law and grace are antithetical terms: "The law was given by Moses—but grace and truth came by Jesus Christ" (John 1:17). It is significant that the word "Gospel" is never found in the Old Testament. Consider a few contrasts between them: The Law manifested what was in man—sin; grace manifests what is in God—love, mercy. The Law speaks of what man must do for God; grace tells of what Christ has done for men. The Law demanded righteousness from men; grace brings righteousness to men. The Law brought out God to men; grace brings in men to God. The Law sentenced a living man to death; grace brings a dead man to life. The Law never had a missionary; the Gospel is to be preached to every creature. The Law makes known the will of God; grace reveals the heart of God!

In the third place, grace, then, is the very opposite of justice. Justice shows no favor and knows no mercy. Grace is the reverse of this. Justice requires that everyone should receive his due; grace bestows on sinners what they are not entitled to—pure charity. Grace is "something for nothing."

Now the Gospel is a revelation of this wondrous grace of God. It tells us that Christ has done for sinners what they could not do for themselves—it satisfied the demands of God's Law. Christ has fully and perfectly met all the requirements of God's holiness so that He can righteously receive every poor sinner who comes to Him. The Gospel tells us that Christ died not for good people, who never did anything very bad; but for lost and godless sinners who never did anything good. The Gospel reveals to every sinner, for his acceptance, a Savior all-sufficient, "able to save unto the uttermost those who come unto God by Him."

The Gospel is a Proclamation of the Grace of God.

The word "Gospel" is a technical one, employed in the New Testament in a double sense: in a narrower, and in a wider one. In its narrower sense, it refers to heralding the glorious fact that the grace of God has provided a Savior for every poor sinner who feels his need, and by faith receives Him. In its wider sense, it comprehends the whole revelation which God made of Himself in and through Christ. In this sense it includes the whole of the New Testament.

Proof of this double application of the term Gospel is found in 1 Corinthians 15:1-3, a definition of the Gospel in its narrower sense: "that Christ died for our sins, was buried, and rose again." Then Romans 1:1 uses the term Gospel in its wider sense: there it includes the whole doctrinal exposition of that epistle. When Christ bade His disciples, "Preach the Gospel to every creature," I do not think He had reference to all that is in the New Testament, but simply to the fact that the grace of God has provided a Savior for sinners. Therefore we say that the Gospel is a proclamation of the grace of God.

The Gospel affirms that grace is the sinner's only hope. Unless we are saved by grace we cannot be saved at all. To reject a gratuitous salvation is to spurn the only one that is available for lost sinners. Grace is God's provision for those who are so corrupt that they cannot change their own natures; so averse to God, they cannot turn to Him; so blind they cannot see Him; so deaf they cannot hear Him; in a word, so dead in sin that He must open their graves and bring them on to resurrection-ground, if ever they are to be saved. Grace, then, implies that the sinner's case is desperate, but that God is merciful.

The Gospel of God's grace is for sinners in whom there is no help. It is exercised by God "without respect of persons," without regard to merit, without requirement of any return. The Gospel is not good advice, but Good

News. It does not speak of what man is to do, but tells what Christ has done. It is not sent to good men, but to bad. Grace, then, is something that is worthy of God.

The Gospel is a Manifestation of the Grace of God.

The Gospel is the "power of God unto salvation to everyone that believes." It is the chosen instrument which God uses in freeing and delivering His people from error, ignorance, darkness, and the power of Satan. It is by and through the Gospel, applied by the Holy Spirit, that His elect are emancipated from the guilt and power of sin. "For the preaching of the cross is to those who perish foolishness; but unto us who are saved it is the power of God . . . But we preach Christ crucified, unto the Jews a stumbling block, and unto the Greeks foolishness; but unto those who are called, both Jews and Greeks, Christ the power of God, and the wisdom of God" (1 Cor. 1:18, 23). Where evolution is substituted for the new birth, the cultivation of character for faith in the blood of Christ, development of will-power for humble dependence on God, the carnal mind may be attracted and poor human reason appealed to, but it is all destitute of power and brings no salvation to the perishing. There is no Gospel in a system of ethics, and no dynamic in the exactions of law.

But grace works. It is something more than a good-natured smile, or a sentiment of pity. It redeems, conquers, saves. The New Testament interprets grace as power. By it redemption comes, for it was by "the grace of God" that Christ tasted death "for everyone" of the sons (Heb. 2:9). Forgiveness of sins is proclaimed through His blood "according to the riches of his grace" (Eph. 1:7). Grace not only makes salvation possible but also effectual. Grace is all-powerful. "My grace is sufficient for you" (2 Cor. 12:9)—sufficient to overcome unbelief, the infirmities of the flesh, the oppositions of men, and the attacks of Satan.

This is the glory of the Gospel: it is the power of God unto salvation. In one of his books, J. H. Jowett says: A little while ago I was speaking to a New York doctor, a man of long and varied experience with diseases that afflict both the body and mind. I asked him how many cases he had known of the slaves of drink having been delivered by medical treatment into health and freedom. How many he had been able to "doctor" into liberty and self-control. He immediately replied, "Not one." He further assured me that he believed his experience would be corroborated by the testimony of the faculty of medicine.

Doctors might afford a temporary escape, but the real bonds are not broken. At the end of the apparent but brief deliverance, it will be found that the chains remain. Medicine might address itself to effects, but the cause is as real and dominant as ever. The doctor has no cure for the drunkard. Medical skill cannot save him. But grace can! Without doctors, drugs, priests, penance, works, money or price, grace actually saves. Hallelujah! Yes, grace saves. It snaps the fetters of a lifetime, and makes a poor sinner a partaker of the divine nature and a rejoicing saint. It saves not only from the bondage of fleshly habits, but also from the curse of the fall, from the captivity of Satan, from the wrath to come.

What effect has this message on your heart? Does it fill you with praise to God? Are you thankful to know that salvation is by grace? Can you see and appreciate the infinite difference between all of man's schemes for self-betterment and the "Gospel of the Grace of God?"

Made in United States
North Haven, CT
16 February 2023